Presented To:

_____

By:

_____

Date:

_____

THE MINISTER'S LITTLE DEVOTIONAL BOOK

by

H. B. London Jr. & Stan Toler

Honor Books
Tulsa, Oklahoma

DEDICATION

To the memory of our fathers:

Holland B. London, Sr.

1908-1996

William Aaron Toler

1926-1962

Special Thanks From H. B. London Jr.

My ability to contribute in some small way to clergy persons who will read this book comes from the many pastors — old and young — who have touched my life, and the untold numbers of parishioners who have trusted me as their spiritual leader.

For my secretary, Sue McFadden, who has worked with me for a quarter of a century; for my wife, Beverly, and our extended family, who have always been patient with me and ever faithful; to Stan Toler, who invited me into this project; and to Dr. James Dobson and Focus on the Family, who have expanded my ability to serve the greater church of Jesus Christ — to all of these, I am indebted and most grateful.

Special Thanks From Stan Toler

To my two minister brothers, Terry and Mark. Your encouragement, prayers, friendship and sense of humor have kept me in the ministry for over 30 years. You are loved!

To Keith Provance, Mona Krewson and the Honor Books family for your "excellence in publishing."

To Jim Wilcox, the one and only Southern Nazarene University "grammar hammer" who's not too bad with a Wilson hammer (racket), either!

To Mark Hollingsworth, Terry Toler, Mechelle Fain, Michael Johnson, Norma Adams, and Jim and Cindi Williams for your assistance, research, and creative help with this project.

Contents

Introduction

We have one main purpose in writing *The Minister's Little Devotional Book*, and that is to help you draw nearer to our Lord, to facilitate that closeness you covet with Him. Our purpose is presented with humility, as we believe ultimately, it is the Holy Spirit who will guide you nearer to Him.

We have all experienced those unmistakable moments when, in the solitude of our own hearts, we can hear God's voice and feel His presence — those inexpressible times when we know He really cares for us. There is a sense that everything is going to be all right. Then there are the unmistakable occasions when "He gives strength to the weary and increases the power of the weak" (Isaiah 40:29) as only He can when we devote time to Him.

It is in those introspective situations, when He seems so near and loving, that we feel free to pray the Psalmist's prayer of confession, "Search me, O God, and know my heart; test me and know my anxious thoughts. See if there is any offensive way in me and lead me in the way everlasting" (Psalm 139:23,24). Instinctively, we know He is sensitive to our plea.

There are also those triumphant moments of exhilaration when we have tasted victory. In our hearts we know we have carried out our assignment in accordance with His will. In the privacy of our time together we can hear His expression of affirmation, *I am well pleased with you.* What a wonderful feeling to know He is happy with us!

We know you are busy, because we have shared your journey. We also know from personal experience, nothing is more energizing and life-changing than times of intimacy with our gracious Father! That is why this book is so important to us.

These devotions contain something for every minister, whether full-time or lay volunteer. You will feel your spirit lift with the humorous anecdotes, discover much needed direction through the scriptures quoted, find encouragement and inspiration from reading the experiences of others, and gain blessed assurance that you are not the only one to face battles. Others have walked through flood and fire to experience victory — and so will you!

More than anything, our prayer is that you will make time each day to read a portion from these pages. Grow quiet enough to hear, "Be still, and know that I am God" (Psalm 46:10), and take that knowledge with you the rest of your day!

THE MINISTER'S LITTLE DEVOTIONAL BOOK

by

H. B. London Jr. & Stan Toler

COURAGE

"'Courage,' he said, and
pointed toward the land,
'this mounting wave will roll
us shoreward soon.'
In the afternoon they
came unto a land...."

Alfred Lord Tennyson

Be strong and courageous.
Do not be afraid or terrified because
of them, for the Lord your God
goes with you; he will never
leave you nor forsake you.

Deuteronomy 31:6

At precisely 9:02 a.m. on April 19, 1995, Oklahoma City, Oklahoma, got a wake-up call — and *courage* went to work. For the next 72 hours, people from all over the world gathered to rescue those who had been trapped from the terrorist bombing of the Alfred P. Murrah Federal Building downtown.

Story after story began to surface of rescuers burrowing deep into the dangerous darkness and precarious pockets of debris — hoping for a pulse and praying for a miracle. Such a miracle occurred late that first evening when the weak cries of Diana Bradley, 21, were heard.

For ten hours she had been pinned beneath the rubble. Choked by dust and numbed by shock, she waited for someone to hear her. Finally relief came, but at a high price. Her leg was caught under large amounts of steel and concrete. Knowing she would die before rescuers could extract her, doctors were called in to amputate. No anesthesia. No attending nurses. No high-speed instruments. Only a doctor with a sharp scalpel.

Three months later to the day Diana, wearing a prosthesis, held a news conference in Oklahoma City. She praised the courage of those who saved her life.

Where do you need courage today? Draw upon the strength of the Holy Spirit within and remember: Courage is a gift from God that enables us to see beyond the moment into the eternal eyes of our heavenly Father.

PERSEVERANCE

"Great works are performed,
not by strength, but
by perseverance."

Samuel Johnson

*Let us run with perseverance
the race marked out for us.*

Hebrews 12:1

A basketball coach tells his players on the first day of practice, "Being in good shape is never measured by how tired you become. It's how fast you recover."

Have you ever noticed friends of yours who are just a bit more persistent than you? When the pink slip arrives, when the car won't start, or when the phone call is bad news, they stand fast and firm as if to say, "If the going gets tough, then I'll get going."

It is gratifying to know that the famous Russian author, Leo Tolstoy, wrote five separate drafts of his masterpiece, *War and Peace,* before it was published. And the American novelist, Ernest Hemingway, rewrote a passage from *A Call To Arms* fifty-one times before he was content. Often, greatness is measured less by talent than by tenacity.

There's a pastor on the West coast who has this saying on a plaque above the desk in his study: "Hangest Thou in There." It's not only his personal motto, it's what he tells people at the altar, in the hospital, and on their worst days. It's not trite to him. It's scriptural and full of promise.

Is there a situation you're facing that is particularly frustrating? Perhaps this is an area where you can develop perseverance! Ask God for new strength to use the difficulties of life to develop an overcoming spirit.

PRIORITIES

"Neglected duties at home disqualify a preacher from ministry in the church."

George McKinney

Choose my instruction instead of silver, knowledge rather than choice gold.

Proverbs 8:10

When my department at *Focus on the Family* conducted a conference for pastors and their spouses, we took a survey. One of the questions asked was, "If you could change one thing that would improve your present situation, what would it be?" Their answers:

1. More family time.
2. A more receptive laity.
3. Better management of time.
4. A regular program of physical exercise.
5. A trustworthy person in whom to confide.

These responses are a reflection of their priorities.

Priorities are frequently ordered by preference. We have our likes and dislikes and we often do what we want to, when we want to. Priorities are also arranged by urgency. The urgency of the problem or dilemma has a way of dictating what matters. Finally, priorities are set by importance — the greatest good for the greatest number.

A college professor in Oklahoma asks everyone he knows and teaches, "What is your philosophy of life?" Most are shocked at such a question, because it asks them to capsulize their priorities a bit too tightly. But it is a good question, for your priorities reflect your philosophy of life.

Would you need to reorder your priorities to live according to your philosophy of life?

REVIVAL

"Hallelujah, Thine the Glory!

Revive us again!"

William P. Mackay

If my people, who are called
by my name, will humble themselves
and pray and seek my face and
turn from their wicked ways, then will
I hear from heaven and will forgive
their sin and will heal their land.

2 Chronicles 7:14

At the dawning of the 20th century, General William Booth of the Salvation Army prophesied the Church would experience the following points of departure if revival did not occur:

Christianity without Christ
Forgiveness without repentance
Salvation without regeneration
Religion without the Holy Spirit
Politics without God
Heaven without hell

Some years ago, a pastor reviewed Booth's words and cried out to God for revival. Finally, in desperation he asked a dear saint, "What will bring revival?" Without hesitation she responded, "2 Chronicles 7:14!"

The next Sunday the pastor spoke from 2 Chronicles 7:14 and shared the following formula for revival: Pray without ceasing. Practice holiness in our living. Love our brothers and sisters. Be diligent in outreach. Demonstrate generosity in our giving. Experience the power of the Holy Spirit.

As the pastor completed his message, people began to move forward, weeping and praying for revival. God truly came into their midst, and the church experienced revival unlike anything they had ever known.

Are you hungry for revival, or are you in a comfortable — or uncomfortable — rut? Why not follow this formula for revival? God wants all His people to be revived daily!

MERCY

"The best exercise for strengthening the heart is reaching down and helping someone up."

L. B. Hicks

If a man's gift...is showing mercy, let him do it cheerfully.

Romans 12:6, 8

O␣ne fall, I observed a beautiful sight while looking out my window. On their southern migration, some geese had chosen the *Focus on the Family* property as a stopping place. Morning and evening they came and went.

After a few days, I noticed a crippled goose. We named him "Chester." He limped along behind the rest and often sat isolated from the others. I watched Chester each day, hoping he would survive another cold night.

I thought of how there are those of us who, for one reason or another, find ourselves limping through a difficult assignment. Yet it seems when we need people most, we tend to isolate ourselves from those who might give us comfort and counsel.

On the other hand, sometimes we see "Chesters" limping along all alone. They cry out for us to look their way and give them a helping hand, but often our inclination is to look or walk the other way. One or more "Chesters" in our crowded world would almost be too much.

The fact is, Jesus is in every "Chester" we meet along the way. "Inasmuch as you have done it unto one of the least of these my brethren, you have done it unto me." Matthew 25:40 KJV. The "Chesters" in our life give us the opportunity to show His mercy and grace.

Identify a "Chester" in your life and ask God to show you the best way to minister to him or her.

PRINCIPLES

"Methods change but
principles never do!"

Elmer Towns

*So David triumphed over
the Philistine with a sling
and a stone.*

1 Samuel 17:50

While planting a church in Florida, one pastor began to focus on what many call the principle-centered life. He turned to the life of David and discovered principles that led him from his lowly role as a shepherd boy to the lofty status as king of Israel.

According to 1 Samuel 17, there were no giant-killers in Saul's army. A review of verses 15-51 reveal the "Top Ten Life-Impacting Principles for Overcoming Giants."

10. Be faithful and responsible in the little assignments (v. 15).
9. Be disciplined and trim off excess baggage (v. 22).
8. Be consumed with the glory of God (v. 26).
7. Be committed in spite of criticism (v. 28).
6. Be happy in the place where you are serving (v. 32).
5. Be ready to point to God's history of faithfulness (vv. 34-37).
4. Be comfortable with your gifts and personality (vv. 38-39).
3. Be confident in everyday battles (vv. 45-47).
2. Be aggressive and decisive when required (v. 48).
1. Be determined to have daily victory over the giants in your life (vv. 49-51).

David became a giant-killer because he practiced the principle-centered life. Make these principles part of your life today!

INSTRUCTION

"Why not resign as General
Manager of the universe
and let God have control?"

*Teach me to do your will, for
you are my God; may your good
Spirit lead me on level ground.*

Psalm 143:10

As a minister you can probably relate to the story President Ronald Reagan often told about the newspaper reporter for the *Los Angeles Times*. He had received instructions from his senior editor to get photographs of a brush fire in the foothills of northern California.

The instructions included hurrying to the Santa Monica Airport to board a small plane, taking some photos of the fire, and hurrying back by noon with the story. (Reporters are always in a hurry to meet their deadlines.)

The reporter dressed quickly, rushed to the airport, saw the small plane waiting on the runway, drove his car to the end of the runway, parked, and climbed on board.

Off they flew into the clear blue skies. At about 5,000 feet, the reporter took out his camera and said to the man flying the plane, "Bank right and I'll take some pictures of this fire." Then he heard the most frightening questions of his life, "Bank right? Why don't you bank right? You're the instructor, aren't you?"

Do you ever feel like you are the instructor and you don't have a clue as to how to do the job? Take a moment to get God's wisdom for the difficult situations you are facing. And remember, He is in control of this universe and nothing takes Him by surprise!

MISSION

"If one's mission is too small, too vague, too parochial, there is the supreme danger of ending up being driven by someone else's mission."

For the Son of Man came to seek and to save what was lost.

Luke 19:10

Organizations, marriages, families, churches, and governments are no stronger than the shared sense of mission that each possess. The mission of your church or ministry is not carried out until that mission is written in the minds of people you lead.

When we use the word *mission,* we are talking about a foundational intention that gives meaning and direction to life. A mission well-articulated will provide guidance to all who adhere to the organization.

Jesus Christ had a mission that He never once walked away from. Even when his closest friends and critics tried to dissuade him, His mission guided His decisions and values.

Jesus' mission? He came to seek and save the lost. Therefore, it is easy to understand why Jesus stopped by the roadside and responded to a blind man's plea, why He spoke to a despised tax collector who climbed a tree, and why He allowed a prostitute to anoint Him with expensive perfume.

In a world where souls drift so easily in the myriad of choices and distractions, we ministers would do well to develop a simple covenant between ourselves and the Father — a covenant describing what His mission for our lives is — and never walk away from it.

What is your mission? Write it down and make certain every one who shares your mission has a copy.

LEADERSHIP

"The sign of a good
follower is that he pushes;
the mark of a great leader
is that she pulls."

John Maxwell

If anyone would come after me,
he must deny himself and take up
his cross daily and follow me.

Luke 9:23

It is part of the American culture: at every commencement ceremony on every college and high school campus in the land, the featured speaker invariably claims to mothers and fathers, "These fine students — your children — are our great leaders of tomorrow."

The trouble is, it's simply not true. Not for 99 percent of them, anyway. Face it — most people don't know the first thing about becoming, much less being, a great leader. Despite what you might read in the latest autobiographies on the bookshelves today, effective leaders are never born — they are made.

If you are asking yourself today, "How can I better lead my people?" perhaps you first ought to ask, "How might I become a humble follower?" Here are six keys.

Failure. A good follower, hence a powerful leader, must risk failure — and grow from it.

Originality. Look for every chance to do things in a new way.

Listen. Nobody has ever learned anything by talking.

Lean. Become dependent on the guidance of the Holy Spirit and seek the counsel of friends and family.

Obedience. It is never a sign of weakness to say "yes" to God.

Willingness. The hardest thing about following is making yourself do whatever needs to be done.

AMBITION

"You make up your mind before you start that sacrifice is a part of the package."

Richard M. DeVos

And everyone who has left houses or brothers or sisters or father or mother or children or fields for my sake will receive a hundred times as much and will inherit eternal life.

Matthew 19:29

I have always marveled at Paul's proclamation that he had "become all things to all men." (See 1 Corinthians 9:22.) Most of us would settle for being something to somebody. Yet, we strive so often to be revered by all, knowing we will fail most of the time.

That ambition has often been referred to as the "walk on the water" syndrome. So often, the people we lead expect the miraculous and we do not want to disappoint them. I nearly destroyed my health trying to "walk on water." As I look back, I have learned the following:

- Know your limits.
- Consider the counsel of others.
- Don't let people put you on a pedestal.
- Make sure you are transparent and confessional.
- Learn the phrase, "I don't know, but I care deeply."
- Encourage your spouse to keep you humble.
- Listen closely to the still small voice of God.
- Remember: Jesus loved all men, but obeyed only His Father — not the urgency of the moment, the push of the crowd, or the whims of His disciples.

You're not a super-being, but you serve a super God whose powerful Holy Spirit dwells within you. Let Him be praised and glorified through you as you do your best to obey and please Him each day.

PERSISTENCE

"Persistence is the ability to
face defeat again and again
without wavering —
to move forward in
the face of great trial."

*I press on toward the goal to win
the prize for which God has called
me heavenward in Christ Jesus.*

Philippians 3:14

Brett Butler is my favorite major leaguer, especially since he became the center-fielder for the Los Angeles Dodgers. He is scrappy, consistent, and the consummate team player. He's a bit undersized for his position, but the greater the odds are against him, the better he plays.

In the middle of the 1996 season, Butler was diagnosed with throat cancer. They said it would end his career, but Butler predicted he would be back before the season ended. Bravely, he endured the radiation, chemotherapy, and physical therapy.

As he predicted, Butler defied the odds and returned to the starting lineup — ready to lead the Dodgers into the playoffs. His first night back, he went one for three and scored the winning run. It was a great victory.

Butler's experience teaches us that, even when things are not going well and challenges take us out of our game, we can still hold our heads high, give God the glory, and be an inspiration to those around us. We cannot let setbacks keep us out of the game!

What is trying to hold you back and keep you out of the game today? Ask God for His strategy to overcome every obstacle and move beyond any failure. Be persistent and press on!

ETERNAL
REWARDS

"You must pay the price if you wish to secure the blessing."

Andrew Jackson

I have fought the good fight, I have finished the race, I have kept the faith. Now there is in store for me the crown of righteousness.

2 Timothy 4:7, 8

In 1996 my father, Holland London, passed away at the age of 88. Converted when he was five years old, it is said that when he was just seven, he would exhort people to come forward and receive Christ during the invitation at campmeetings. He was called to the ministry when he was nine and held his first revival effort when he was only 16.

He served as superintendent and pastor in the Church of the Nazarene in his early adult life, and later became the president of California Graduate School of Theology, where he touched the lives of hundreds of pastors. He spoke in the most prestigious churches in America, but felt just as comfortable preaching to a few. He was kind and tender in the pulpit, full of wit and humor, but preached a rugged uncompromising truth. I have seen and heard most preachers of his time, but have never seen a man who could "draw the net" like my dad.

A few months before he died, little by little the life he loved became a distant memory. His thoughts turned to a new and brighter home. Today, I am comforted by the fact that Dad is happy there. I have no doubt his rewards are beyond what he ever thought or imagined in this life.

The scripture tells us that keeping an eternal perspective helps us win the battles here on earth. (See 2 Timothy 2:4.) By the way, when was the last time you became a child and let your imagination wander through heaven with Jesus?

CHOICES

"The greatest power
a person possesses is
the power to choose."

*Delight yourself in the Lord and he
will give you the desires of your heart.*

Psalm 37:4

A recent birthday caused me to reflect and look back over much of my professional life. Certain questions came to my mind. *Should I have done things differently? What would I change about my lifestyle?*

These are my conclusions. First, I would have studied more. Second, I would have been more faithful in my quiet time with the Lord. Third, I would have been a better listener. (So often in ministry we feel inclined to "talk our way through.")

Fourth, I would have given more attention to the present and a lot less time bemoaning the past or fretting over tomorrow, for I missed a lot of "happy days." And last, I would have spent much more time with my family. When you pause to think about it, they matter more than anyone.

If I were to add one more, it would probably be to take myself less seriously. If you have not already noticed, none of us are indispensable or infallible.

As I re-read these thoughts, it occurs to me that it's not too late! I trust these days are going well for you, but please slow down and ask yourself what *you* would do differently.

It never hurts to take time off periodically and reassess your daily, monthly, and yearly goals. This will help you keep your priorities straight and stay focused on what God has called you to do.

KINDNESS

"If you can't say anything
nice about someone,
don't say anything at all."

Every Mom

*Do not forget to entertain
strangers, for by so doing
some people have entertained
angels without knowing it.*

Hebrews 13:2

Ron had long hair when it stood for "rebel," listened to heavy-metal music, drank alcohol, and experimented with drugs. He had also tried church but had been "turned off" by the zeal of a few and the judgmental eyes of others.

One summer he was hired to work in a lumber yard in California. He was partnered with a skinny, fair-skinned Christian teenager named Joe, who immediately thought Ron was "cool."

Over the weeks, Ron and Joe laughed, ate, and talked for eight hours a day. Ron drilled Joe about God and the Gospel, but Joe never pretended to know all the answers. One day, Joe asked Ron if he'd like to come over to his house — a beautiful home — for dinner the next night.

A couple of weeks later, Ron got brave enough to ask Joe over to his small house in a poor neighborhood, where he introduced Joe to some of his favorite music.

As the summer drew to a close and Joe prepared to return to college, they both knew that their days together at the lumber yard were numbered. As they walked out to the car on Ron's last day, he looked up at Joe and tearfully said, "A lot of people have tried to tell me about Jesus, but Joe, you're the first person who has shown Him to me."

Kindness is a habit you never want to break! Is it one of yours? If not, why not begin cultivating it today? Ask God to show you who needs your kindness and how you can demonstrate it to them.

UNCTION

"In too many places,
the bland pulpit has called
for its own demise."

Grant Swank

*THE SPIRIT of the Sovereign
Lord is on me, because the Lord
has anointed me to preach....*

Isaiah 61:1

A favorite course in seminary is The History of
Preaching. Preacher wannabes love studying great
sermons like "Sinners in the Hands of an Angry God,"
by Jonathan Edwards.

A preacher said that as a young man he often heard
the older ministers talk about *unction*. It mystified and at
times confused him in his early attempts to preach the
Gospel.

What is unction? A candidate for ordination was
asked by the credentials committee, "Would you be
disgusted if we didn't ordain you this year?"

"Oh no," replied the man, "God has already
ordained me. He's just waiting for you all to get the
paperwork done!"

Unction to preach the Word comes from Above.

How do you experience divine unction each time
you minister? The following spiritual exercises will help
you reach a "God-moment" the next time you preach or
teach:

1. Seek the mind of God in sermon preparation.
2. Pray for the presence of God in your worship
   service.
3. Invite prayer partners to pray before you preach.
4. Look to the Word of God as your ultimate
   source.
5. Be sensitive and obedient to the leading of the
   Holy Spirit before, during, and after you deliver
   the message.

VISION

"Visionary leadership will challenge the people of God."

Talmadge Johnson

*Where there is not vision,
the people perish.*

Proverbs 29:18 KJV

Rick Warren led his great church from infancy to 10,000 in attendance — in 15 short years. How? Rick Warren is a visionary leader! By his own admission, "God gave me a vision to build a purpose-driven church."

Most pastors are not like Rick Warren. In fact, many pastors struggle with the so-called "vision" thing. But every pastor who is making a difference in his community has a sense of destiny that is driven by the leadership of the Holy Spirit.

Vision is a key to making an impact for God in an unholy world.

Perhaps these simple steps will assist you in your search for a vision from God:

Spend time daily in prayer, asking God for the vision for your church or ministry.

Study the needs of your surrounding community or the people God has called you to reach.

Seek wise counsel from visionary leaders.

Examine your resources.

Accept what God reveals to you and share it with your followers.

Henrietta Mears once said, "There is no magic in small plans. When I consider my ministry, I think of the world. Anything less than that would not be worthy of Christ nor of His will for my life."

Think BIG! God does!

HARVEST

"While the world has been multiplying, the church has been making additions."

D. James Kennedy

The harvest is plentiful but the workers are few.

Matthew 9:37

Several years ago, while pastoring in a small Ohio farming community, Rev. Blake Willingham became concerned about the need for a spiritual harvest. It was during a missions conference that he opened his heart to serve as a missionary.

After much prayer, he realized God wanted him to see the world in the light of Matthew 9 and become a "sending pastor" rather than a foreign missionary.

The next year he traveled to Kenya, Africa, and observed the plight of the Masai warriors. He then traveled to Bolivia and met with missionaries on the edge of the Amazon jungle. He went on to India, with its poverty and spiritual darkness, and also to the inner cities of the United States.

When his "missionary journey" was completed, he was a different pastor. He had a new view of the world!

It was only after seeing the need for the Gospel first-hand that he began to fully comprehend what Jesus meant when he said, "Go and make disciples of all nations."

When Rev. Willingham responded to the call of Christ in Matthew 9, he became a sending pastor. What is God saying to you about the need for a harvest of souls in your sphere of service?

Take steps today to begin carrying out God's mandate for winning the lost through your ministry.

SERVANTHOOD

"Service is an act;
Servanthood is a lifestyle."

LeBron Fairbanks

*The Son of Man did not come
to be served, but to serve.*

Matthew 20:28

Mary and Don were two of the funniest people in the world. Their marriage was full of laughter and love for each other and for those around them. Then one day Don went out one snowy morning to shovel the sidewalk for his next door neighbor. He suffered a fatal heart attack, and Mary was left alone in their home that had echoed for more than 30 years with such great joy.

A group of college students from Mary's church adopted her as their own grandmother. For the next year they dropped by to visit, shopped for her groceries, took care of her yard, maintained her car, and gently made sure she knew they were around. She told everyone they were her "angels."

It is easy to love others on paper. It is quite another thing to show the love of God to someone who needs desperately to see it. It takes work. It takes money. *It takes time.*

When we become Christians, Jesus calls us to be like Him, and Jesus got involved with people — not just by addressing the multitude from the mountaintop, but face-to-face and one-on-one.

Are you serving only from a pulpit? If so, you are stunting your growth and depriving yourself of tremendous joy. Pray for opportunities to serve people in special and unusual ways. You will never be the same!

EXAMPLE

"God of goodness, give me
Yourself, for You are
sufficient for me."

Julian of Norwich

*Now this is eternal life: that they
may know you, the only true God,
and Jesus Christ, whom you have sent.*

John 17:3

Several years ago at the National Association of Religious Broadcasters meeting, Dr. Richard Halverson, Chaplain of the U. S. Senate, told this most insightful story.

It seems his small son was playing in the backyard with his friends when the conversation turned to one of those "my dad can whip your dad" routines. Halverson overheard one boy say, "My dad knows the mayor of our city!" Another said, "That's nothing — my dad knows the governor of our state!" Then Halverson heard his son say, "That's nothing — my dad knows God!"

Dr. Halverson reported that he slipped away from his place of eavesdropping with hot tears streaming down his cheeks. When he reached his study, he fell on his knees and earnestly prayed, "Oh, God, I pray that my boy will always be able to say, 'My dad knows God.'"

How important it is for us to be a spiritual example for our children, the same example Jesus was for His disciples and for us. He did nothing without the Father. He spent hours in prayer, garnering strength, courage, and wisdom to do the Father's will. Clearly, he showed us how to know God.

If you want to know God more intimately, follow Jesus' example. Establish your own "mountain of prayer," a special time and place to be alone with Him each day.

ATTITUDE

"My heart leaps up when I
behold a rainbow in the sky:
so was it when my life began;
so is it now I am a man;
so be it when I shall grow old,
or let me die!"

William Wordsworth

*Your attitude should be the same
as that of Christ Jesus.*

Philippians 2:5

In his book, *Carpe Diem,* Tony Campolo relates the story of Ralph, a friend of his from the 1960's, whom he met while working in the fair housing movement. Though Ralph came from a Quaker background, he was not a born-again Christian. He didn't mind working with those who were, however.

While Ralph worked in the name of social justice, Tony and his fellow Christians worked in the name of Jesus. Ralph had an attitude to make people comfortable; the Christians had an attitude to show the eternal love and salvation of Jesus.

"The sense of unity we evangelicals felt with Ralph as we worked with him and followed his wise counsel soon became both deep and dynamic. As we struggled with issues, tried to heal one another's wounds, and sought spiritual guidance in establishing strategies for action, little by little Ralph became infected with our faith," Campolo writes.

Years later, Tony and Ralph met again, this time in a church where Ralph now worshipped. Ralph was as active as ever with the social concerns of his community, but now he sought to help others with an attitude to show the lost the reality of God.[1]

Serve your fellowman as Jesus served, and everyone who comes in contact with you will have an encounter with God, just as Ralph did.

EFFECTIVENESS

"Holiness is as essential to
the spiritual life as food is
to the physical life."

R. S. Taylor

*Made holy, useful to the Master
and prepared to do any good work.*

2 Timothy 2:21

A preacher was speaking in the inner city when a church deacon interrupted the service to tell the congregation that vandals had smashed several car windows and someone needed to call the police.

The pastor responded, "No, we're not calling the police; we need to fall on our knees and ask God to forgive us for not being more effective in reaching the gangs in this community."

What an example of holiness at work!

The Word of God clearly links holiness with effectiveness. The reality is, we cannot bring our service to God in unclean vessels.

The One who makes us effective in the premarital counseling session, in the hospital intensive care unit, at the graveside of a stillborn child, in the pulpit, and in the serving of the sacraments, is the Holy Spirit.

With the Holy Spirit's power flowing through our lives, we are "prepared to do any good work!" (See 2 Timothy 2:21.) He is the One who makes us effective in service. And He is *holy*.

Ask Him to show you any area of your life that needs to be purified and set right with God. Don't let any sin, fault, or weakness hold you back from all God wants to accomplish through you!

CONSISTENCY

"Lord, help me to show my
children your ways."

David Vaughn

*Jesus Christ is the same
yesterday and today and forever.*

Hebrews 13:8

As I wind my father's old watch, it is my prayer that I will live out the great lessons of life he shared with me. My friend, Jim Wilcox, reflects for me:

NOW

Then, I thought Dad was teaching me to ride a
 bike without training wheels;
Now, I know he was showing me how to stand on
 my own two feet.
Then, I thought he was teaching me to construct a
 kite out of newspaper and an old yardstick;
Now, I realize that he was encouraging me to fly.
Then, I thought he was forcing me to eat
 everything on my plate;
Now, I realize he was teaching me the integrity of
 commitment.
Then, I thought he was coaching me to throw and
 catch a baseball;
Now, I realize he was telling me that those who
 play together stay together.
Then, I thought he was helping me finish my math
 homework for tomorrow;
Now, I realize he was teaching me that learning
 lasts a lifetime.
Then, I thought he was working for a living;
Now, I realize he was working for me and leaving
 giant footprints to follow.

RESPONSIBILITY

"The ability to accept
responsibility is the
measure of a man."

Roy L. Smith

*Watch your life and doctrine closely.
Persevere in them, because if you do,
you will save both yourself
and your hearers.*

1 Timothy 4:16

I read a survey stating that four out of five of those who sit in the pew at church expect their pastor and his family to live at a higher level of moral integrity than other people. The survey went on to say that few of them thought any minister would be able to measure up!

While this may be hard for us to hear, realistically it is the world we live in.

From time to time, political scandals erupt, from the local level all the way to the national level. Scandals and wrongdoings on a local level can be somewhat tolerated. However, scandals linked to the White House, the highest office in the land, are more difficult to accept.

The world watches the church and its leadership in much the same way we all watch the White House. Having higher expectations, we don't give our president much room for error — and neither should we expect to receive much slack from those who follow us! In short, the world is watching us.

Make an honest assessment of the standard you adhere to in word and deed, and ask God to reveal any area where you may be coming up short. Although it is not the world you are trying to impress or please, but your heavenly Father, as you please Him, you are sure to have a life-changing impact on those around you.

FEARS

"When I have fears that
I may cease to be

Before my pen has glean'd
my teeming brain...

And think that I may
never live to trace

Their shadows...then
on the shore

Of the wide world
I stand alone...."

John Keats

*The Lord is my light and my
salvation — whom shall I fear?*

Psalm 27:1

Dear minister friend, did you know that the number one fear in the world today is speaking in public? (And to think you may do that two or three times a week, you daredevil!)

We are born with only a handful of instinctive fears, and most of them are healthy, — the fear of falling, for example. As we grow older, we discover fears that exploit our emotions: the dentist's drill, the cold doorknob, the child who misses curfew, and the loud bang upstairs.

It is when our fears begin to take control of our lives that we need to take action. At that point, fears are called phobias and ought to be addressed through counseling — or maybe a few parachute jumps from a small bi-plane!

Fear is usually founded in the unknown and grounded in ignorance of God and His Word. It is the opposite of faith, and the Bible says that faith grows as we hear God's Word. (See Romans 10:17.) Therefore, the best way to handle it may be good counsel, exhaustive study, and fervent prayer. Ask God to reveal the cause of your fear and empower you to deal with it resourcefully.

Why not release your fears to the Lord right now? Remember, you are not alone. Your heavenly Father understands and cares, and He is committed to your spiritual tranquillity. After all, he sent Jesus, the Prince of Peace, so you could enjoy the peace that passes all understanding! (See Philippians 4:7.)

DOUBT

"A positive thought is the seed of a positive result."

I know whom I have believed, and am persuaded that he is able to keep that which I have committed unto him against that day.

2 Timothy 1:12 KJV

My Utmost for His Highest is a great book to read every year or two. In this marvelous devotional, Oswald Chambers asks the question, "Have I been doubting something about Jesus?"[2]

One of the twelve, Thomas, refused to believe in the resurrection until he saw the nail prints in the hands and feet of his Messiah. But the truth is, all the disciples doubted Jesus had been raised from the dead.

Quite frequently in ministry, many of us have encountered people plagued by doubt. If we were truthful, we would all have to admit we have struggled with it. Maybe we have wondered if we were centered in God's will. Or perhaps we find ourselves mired in questions the morning after a service.

Perhaps this formula for overcoming doubt will help:

1. Review God's faithfulness throughout your life.
2. Check your attitude — are you walking in faith?
3. Look to Scripture and meditate on God's promises to you.
4. Look within and draw upon the Holy Spirit.
5. Claim 1 John 5:11, 12 — And this is the testimony: God has given us eternal life, and this life is in his Son. He who has the Son has life.

REMEMBERING — TO FORGET

"God forgives and forgets!
Wise is the man or woman
who will do the same."

*Their sins and lawless acts
I will remember no more.*

Hebrews 10:17

Everyday we have the opportunity to remember. We can look back over the preceding day and see that God's faithfulness is tangible: The beautiful sunrise over the neighboring lake. The merging lines of geese honking overhead. The bountiful feast on the dinner table. The quiet night of peaceful slumber.

Meditate on the word, *remember*, and you'll discover it doesn't quite fit God in all ways. In light of His mercy and grace, the word *remember* seems out of place and barren. Think about it for a moment and you'll become very aware of the fact that the Lord doesn't remember some things.

God said, "I will remember their sins no more." Incredible! No wonder this word seems out of place. God doesn't just forgive, He forgets. And there's more! He wipes the slate clean. He destroys all the evidence. *He doesn't remember!*

In the ministry, we are surrounded by people who have been devastated by sin. They can neither forgive themselves nor others, nor can they forget past wrongs. That's why we've been called to serve. People need to know that God's memory is short, that He's long on grace.

Today you may meet someone who is having a difficult time forgiving themselves for some past failure. Remind them of God's "forgetful nature." And if you need to, remind yourself to forget!

PARENTING

"There is just one way to bring up a child in the way he should go and that is to travel that way yourself."

Abraham Lincoln

Train a child in the way he should go, and when he is old he will not turn from it.

Proverbs 22:6

A pastor came home from a tough day at the office and said to his wife, "I've had a bad day. Please, if you have any bad news, keep it to yourself." To which she replied, "Okay. No bad news. Now for the good news. Remember our four children? Well, three of them didn't break an arm today."

Parenting is an overwhelming responsibility. The older our children become, the more overwhelmed we can become. We often feel like a short-legged beagle chasing a rabbit in a foot of snow!

As a parent, we're to *provide* for our children and *protect* our children, but our most important parenting responsibility is to *point* our children to Christ.

I WANT MY CHILDREN TO REMEMBER:

Mom and Dad love each other.

Home is a happy place to be.

We love people.

I am the apple of God's eye. (See Zechariah 2:8.)

If you are married and have children, take a moment to evaluate your schedule. Can you have lunch with your spouse a set time every week? Are there days when you can pick the kids up at school, help them with homework, and celebrate at the ice cream store?

Pray and ask God to show you how you can improve your family life by being like Jesus to those you love the most.

GUIDANCE

"A journey of a
thousand miles begins
with the first step."

*Since we live by the Spirit,
let us keep in step with the Spirit.*

Galatians 5:25

A traveling minister in a strange town asked a small boy for directions to the post office. After receiving instructions, he thanked the boy. "You seem to be a bright young man. How would you like to come hear me preach tonight? I'm gonna tell people how to get to heaven!"

The boy responded, "You're going to tell people how to get to heaven and you don't even know how to get to the post office?"

Our journey of faith takes us in many directions. Add to that journey of faith the call to ministry and immediately you're on the scenic route!

In Psalm 143, David models a prayer that we must pray frequently to keep in step with the Holy Spirit and follow His direction for our lives. David realized that to know God's direction, he must *listen*. "Point out the road I must travel; I'm all ears, all eyes before you" (Psalm 143:8 The Message).

David also realized the need to *learn*. "Teach me how to live to please you, because you're my God. Lead me by your blessed Holy Spirit into cleared and level pasture-land" (Psalm 143:10 The Message).

Learning God's direction for our lives is a process — an education that never ceases unless we stop listening and learning. Are you listening to *Him* as you go about your day? Are you learning *His* ways in all you do?

PRAYER

"A prayerless preacher is
a powerless preacher."

Mark Hollingsworth

*The shepherds are senseless and
do not inquire of the Lord;
so they do not prosper and
all their flock is scattered.*

Jeremiah 10:21

Peter Wagner surveyed 572 pastors across America regarding their prayer lives. The average amount of time these pastors spent in prayer each day was 22 minutes. He found that 57 percent prayed less than 20 minutes daily, 34 percent spent between 20 minutes and one hour in prayer, but only 9 percent prayed for an hour or longer every day.

There are a number of reasons that churches do not grow — location, denominationalism, sacred cows, poor facilities, etc. But perhaps the most logical reason is located in Jeremiah 10:21. Prayerlessness!

Hudson Taylor said, "The power of prayer has never been fully tried in any church. If we want to see the mighty wonders of divine grace and power, instead of weakness, failure and disappointment, the whole church must accept God's standing challenge: 'Call unto me, and I will answer thee, and show thee great and mighty things, which thou knowest not.'" (See Jeremiah 33:3 KJV.)

Jesus taught us to pray for a reason — to tap into the matchless grace, the magnificent promises, and the marvelous resources of Almighty God. Why? Not only are we equipped to fulfill the call, but we *are fulfilled.*

Don't go another day without assessing your prayer life and making changes. Even if your ministry is thriving, no minister ever prayed too much or experienced "too much of God!"

COMPROMISE

"The man who always has
to be right rarely is."

*Settle matters quickly with your
adversary who is taking you to court.*

Matthew 5:25

A pastor in the Midwest who was known as a great leader often told his congregations that he would not go to battle with them. "I am not a fighter," he told them, "I'm a lover." Is it any surprise that his churches grew and flourished under such a philosophy?

Rhetoricians teach that persuasion is less an art of coercion than it is the art of compromise. Resolution of most arguments is found in the middle of the two points of view rather than in either point alone.

When we speak of compromise, we are not saying you should compromise God's Word! But one of the troubling trends in our society is that we look at *personal* compromise as spiritual and emotional weakness, rather than its true position of strength and power. Finding a peaceful resolution in the center of conflict is the true measure of effective leadership and personal integrity.

Pastors who can mediate, moderate, and compromise will grow churches. Pastors who refuse to budge will fail, because essentially they have chosen to entertain only their point of view.

What conflicts are you involved in currently? Have you taken the time to listen to all viewpoints and consider all positions? Remember, Jesus told us that peacemakers were blessed! (See Matthew 5:9.) Take every opportunity to stop a war and be a peacemaker.

UNITY

"Tying two cats' tails together
does not necessarily
constitute unity."

*I have given them the glory
you gave me — the glorious unity
of being one, as we are.*

John 17:22, 23 TLB

There once was a church that had little unity. In spite of their inability to get along, however, they reached thousands of people for Christ.

Although they were effective in outreach, this church experienced overwhelming obstacles. The church treasurer ran off with the church's money. The leaders of the church were constantly making people mad. The associate pastor was impulsive and quick to put his foot in his mouth.

Finally, a crisis came and the church divided. Several members were forced to attend churches in other cities because the persecution was so great.

Where was this church? It was the church in Jerusalem! They would have done well to follow these tips to develop unity:

Keep your tongue bridled.

Keep your promises.

Praise more often than criticize.

Value people more than things.

Smile frequently.

Discuss without arguing.

Refuse to gossip.

Laugh with people, never at them.

With these standards for your ministry, how can you go wrong?

COUNSEL

"Happy is the minister
who finds counsel in the
presence of the Lord."

*Plans fail for lack of counsel,
but with many advisers they succeed.*

Proverbs 15:22

Being a minister is not an easy assignment! Thankfully, Jesus is the Wonderful Counselor, not just for the people we lead, but for ourselves and our families. Every word of Isaiah 9:6, 7 penetrates deeply into our being, reminding us that the God of the universe is reachable and intimately involved in our lives.

It is said that God's power was always evident wherever Robert Murray McCheyne spoke. He was one of the great Scottish preachers of the 19th century, and everywhere he stepped, Scotland shook.

A minister went to the hometown of McCheyne, hoping to see where he had preached. An elderly gentleman escorted him to McCheyne's study and asked him to sit in McCheyne's chair. The man hesitated for a moment, then sat down. On the table was an open Bible. The tour guide said, "Drop your head on that book and weep. That's what McCheyne did before he went out to preach."

We would do well to heed the admonition of the elderly gentleman. Seeking God's counsel from His Word will not only strengthen us on a daily basis, but will be the life we impart to others as we preach, teach, and counsel others.

Be honest — do you spend enough time praying over God's Word and seeking deeper revelation on truth from the Holy Spirit? If so, by all means continue and become even more fervent. If not, do something about it today!

EVANGELISM

"We are debtors to give the Gospel in the same manner we have received it."

P. F. Bresee

I am not ashamed of the gospel, because it is the power of God for the salvation of everyone who believes: first for the Jew, then for the Gentile.

Romans 1:16

The words of Bill Waldrop haunt us today: "Over 40 percent of the five billion plus persons on planet earth have never heard of Jesus Christ and never will unless the Church recognizes its unfinished task."

One of the distinguishing characteristics of an effective church is that it places a high priority on reaching the lost. Only the minister who knows God personally can effectively share the importance of witnessing.

One of the great Sunday School teachers of years gone by, Edith Shook, led her charges to the throne of Christ through the simple ABC plan:

Admit you have sinned. (Romans 3:23)

Believe that Jesus Christ can save you. (John 1:12)

Confess that He is Lord of your life. (Romans 10:9, 10)

Many ministers have encouraged parishioners to do the following:

Pray daily for lost friends.

Invite lost friends to fun-filled activities.

Testify of God's faithfulness in your life.

Invite friends to church for an event designed to reach unbelievers.

Share the ABC plan.

Evangelism is not an option for Christians; it is a command! More importantly, it is exciting to know God is using you as a member of His "rescue squad."

COMPASSION

"Compassionate ministry is
done one way: one-on-one,
with all your might,
soul, and mind."

Steve Weber

*I tell you the truth, whatever
you did for one of the least of
these brothers of mine, you did for me.*

Matthew 25:40

It was one of those windy, blustery November days in Oklahoma when everyone looks for the warmest place to hide. The ice on the ground made driving hazardous and the vengeful sleet seemed to punch holes in each brave face that walked the streets.

The pastor of a local congregation had promised to take two college students to the City Rescue Mission that afternoon. So off the three of them went in the pastor's old Buick. Little did he know how the afternoon would change him forever.

Kyle and Brad were two of the soft-hearts of the regional university and not yet acclimated to the brutally cold weather. They had bundled up well for the excursion, which included a brand new sweater for Brad.

After a couple of hours stuffing envelopes for a fundraising campaign, they were treated to a warm broth and white bread lunch, plus a tour of the facility. As they were getting ready to leave the shelter and head back into the cold, the pastor noticed Brad lagging behind. When Brad finally met them outside, he was wearing only a light T-shirt.

"What happened to you?" Kyle asked.

"I just couldn't leave with so much when they had so little," he answered.

How often are you moved with compassion to the point of self-sacrifice? If your answer is "Not often," try seeing every person you meet through God's eyes.

STUDY

"Studying is like a pot of homemade chili. It must simmer for hours to become delicious."

Study to show thyself approved unto God, a workman that needeth not to be ashamed, rightly dividing the word of truth.

2 Timothy 2:15 KJV

We live in a microwave society, and ministry today is often synonymous with "hurry!" We hurry from appointment to appointment, meeting to meeting, and game to game, with little regard for our nutritional needs. If we're not driving "thru" some restaurant, then we are probably shoving some box of painted-on-food into the "zapper."

This generation has failed to understand the value of slowness, meditation, pondering, and wondering. Several years ago, 50 people over the age of 90 were asked what they might do differently if they could live their lives over again. One of the most common responses was, "I would reflect more." Our goal today is more like, "How much can I cram into my schedule?"

Colleges particularly reflect that very way of life. There are precious few *students* on most campuses these days. Most of those who attend universities would be better labeled *crammers*. They don't study a subject — they cram for exams. They have never been taught that study is gradual, intentional, and purposeful.

Knowing God's Word doesn't come through cramming; it comes through deliberate and mindful study and waiting on Him. Don't hurry through your study time with the Lord. There are so many nuggets of gold He is waiting to show you.[3]

GREED

"Don't worry — be happy."

Bobby McFerrin

Whoever trusts in his riches will fall, but the righteous will thrive like a green leaf.

Proverbs 11:28

Russian legend has it that there once was a man who lived in dire poverty. One day he heard of a faraway place that would change his life forever — a place of land, food, and wealth.

He found the leader of these generous people. "Welcome," said the leader. "All that you see is yours." The poor man could not believe his ears nor his eyes, for what he saw was greater than he ever could have imagined.

"How might I acquire a piece of land for myself?" the man asked.

"Tomorrow," he said, "when the sun comes up, you will be given four sharp sticks. From a prescribed starting point you may walk or run and stake out the territory for your new home. The only condition is that you must return to that same starting point before the sun falls below the opposite horizon. If you do not, then you gain nothing."

The next day the poor man walked and ran and dreamed and planned all day, planting the first three stakes miles apart. When he noticed the sun setting, he began to hurry, racing the sun, but his greed prevented him from winning the race. Exhausted to death, he was buried the next morning.

When the leader asked his people, "How much land does a man need? " they replied wisely, "Six feet...and no more."

HUMOR

"Finding humor in almost
any church problem
has kept me sane."

Stan Toler

A cheerful heart is good medicine.

Proverbs 17:22

You Might Be A Preacher If...

...your two-car garage has ever doubled as a Sunday School classroom.

...you've ever received a gift certificate from U-Haul.

...you've ever waded into a creek with a neck-tie.

...you find negotiating with a terrorist easier than negotiating with the church organist.

...you've ever wanted to give the sound man a little feedback of your own.

...you're leading the church into the 21st century, but don't know what you're preaching on Sunday.

...you've ever carried on a conversation with someone on a bed pan.

...a church picnic is no picnic.

...the local undertaker brings you a ham and a calendar every year.

...you wish people would stop honking and start driving if they really love Jesus.

...you've had roast for Sunday dinner.

...Vacation Bible School is no vacation.[4]

CHANGE

"The more things change,
the more they stay the same."

*There is a time for everything, and a
season for every activity under heaven*

Ecclesiastes 3:1

Are you a person who loves change? Or does the very idea of altering the way it's always been send cold chills up and down your spine — especially if it wasn't your idea?

Whatever your reaction, know this truth — *change is going to happen.* It is inevitable and unavoidable, so there's no sense fighting every change that arises. The secret to effective and productive change is found in the first eight verses of Ecclesiastes 3. Read them today.

There is a story of the new pastor who, on his first Sunday, preached before any singing took place. Then, instead of passing offering plates in the pews, he asked his congregation to parade across the front of the sanctuary and drop checks and change into a giant pot. But the most shocking change of all came after the service was over. Instead of greeting his people in the foyer, he exited out the back door and raced them all to the cafeteria. He was changing too much too fast, and it wasn't long until he himself was asked to change churches!

Adjusting to changes in life may be the most difficult thing we have to do. There is almost always a sense of denial and anger before there is acceptance — similar to the grieving process. However, your confidence is in knowing God has your life in the palm of His hands. He is in control, and whatever changes are in store for you, He will always be there to guide you and strengthen you.

DISCIPLINE

"Two roads diverged in a wood, and I — I took the one less traveled by, and that has made all the difference."

Robert Frost

Endure hardship as discipline; God is treating you as sons.

Hebrews 12:7

In sports, there's a thing called "two-a-days" — and no one likes "two-a-days!" Athletes are forced to rise early and practice all morning, running sprints, drills, and exercises until they don't know if they will find enough oxygen in the air to survive. Then, after a few hours of recuperation, they come back for a practice made even more strenuous by the heat of the day in the late afternoon. It is not the coach's intention to kill his players, but to hone them, prepare them, and enable them to excel.

Although extremely tough for the moment, each athlete knows this rigorous training will give them the edge. A disciplined athlete will not only go through this once, but will return day after day for more! They will be ready for each contest and they will succeed.

Discipline creates disciples. In fact, the two words come from the same Latin root, *discipulus*. One cannot, therefore, become a disciple without being disciplined.

Discipline is not a negative term as so many think. We discipline our children because we *love* them. God disciplines us because He *loves* us. Proper discipline is the balance of correction and praise.

It is the wise leader, the effective coach, the loving parent, and the Christ-like minister, who imparts necessary discipline into the lives of others.

CHARACTER

"Someone once asked banker J. P. Morgan what the best collateral was for a loan, and he replied, 'character.'"

For the eyes of the Lord range throughout the earth to strengthen those whose hearts are fully committed to him.

2 Chronicles 16:9

A *Newsweek* article stated, "From the East side of Manhattan to West L.A., Americans are agreeing that there are universally accepted precepts of good character...and that society is failing to teach them anymore."

I am so impressed with Warren Wiersbe's book, *On Being A Servant of God*. On the subject of character, he wrote, "Life is built on character, but character is built on decisions. The decisions you make, small or great, do to your life what the sculptor's chisel does to a block of marble. You are shaping your life by your thoughts, attitudes and actions, and becoming either more or less like Jesus Christ."

Wiersbe goes on to say, "We as God's servants, are standing on holy ground and had better behave accordingly. If nobody else is watching, God is, and He will be our judge."[5]

Character does matter! What is to blame for the decline in morals and personal character in America today? The breakdown of the family was cited in 77 percent of those surveyed.

As a minister, you can influence husbands and wives, fathers and mothers, and children of all ages. The church must be one source that does make a difference. We must set the example of God's standard in a world that desperately needs to see character in action.

HEALTH

"Healthy is he who has learned how to smile."

Do you not know that your body is a temple of the Holy Spirit, who is in you, whom you have received from God?

1 Corinthians 6:19

Are you battling the three B's of middle-age: bifocals, bulges, and baldness?

The secret to health — whether it is physical well-being, spiritual vitality, emotional stability, or psychological security is a fourth B — *balance*.

One who focuses all his attention on physical health to the neglect of other facets of his life, as might be evidenced by models, weight lifters, and hypochondriacs, can become self-centered and have little tolerance for those who are sick, challenged, or obese.

Those, on the other hand, who concentrate solely on their intelligence, spiritual welfare, or emotional survival, may very well end up one of the sick, challenged, or obese. The key is to do all things with moderation and balance.

Instead of looking at health as the constant battle of the bulge — the all-lettuce diet, followed by 750 sit-ups, followed by an all-liquid diet, followed by the New York Marathon — view it as stewardship. Just as you would never neglect the care and upkeep of your church's sanctuary, treat your spirit-temple with equal reverence.

Little credence is given the minister who preaches condemnation of the vices when he is resting his belly on the pulpit!

COMMUNION

"Oh, what sweet communion
I enjoy through the day!"

Terry Toler

*And he took bread, gave thanks and
broke it, and gave it to them, saying,
"This is my body given for you;
do this in remembrance of me."*

Luke 22:19

Partaking of Holy Communion has become a time of contemplation for me, but it was not always a time of introspection. In fact, I was much like my small, six-year-old niece, Mariah Dawn, who whispered to her mother at a communion service, "I love it when we have these little snacks at church!"

Although I have grown spiritually, I must confess that I still have that youthful exuberance as I approach the time of Holy Communion. I have moved from *anticipating* the little snacks as a child to *feasting* on thoughts of what Jesus accomplished through His death on the cross, subsequent burial, and triumphant resurrection from the grave!

Today when we gather at the table, I marvel at the oneness of the family of God eating together at the Table of Remembrance. Oh, what sweet fellowship and communion we enjoy together!

More importantly, one day we will move from the "little snack time" to celebrating with Jesus at the great Marriage Supper of the Lamb. And what a family time that will be!

In the meantime, we can remember Jesus, worship Him, and enjoy His presence not only during Holy Communion in church, but every day, all day long!

UNIQUENESS

"You are an original. God has shaped you for ministry."

H. Norman Wright

I was not disobedient to the vision from heaven.

Acts 26:19

Dr. Charles Crow often says, tongue-in-cheek, "God loves you...but people have a wonderful plan for your life." Often in ministry we have "plans" or "visions" that others thrust upon us. Sometimes, we unwisely attempt to "import" the plans and visions of other successful ministers, usually without success.

You must understand that God is a *personal* God. He has a vision for you just as He has a vision for the minister next door. He's unique and His vision for your ministry is unique.

In the physical realm, we wouldn't think of borrowing a friend's eyeglasses to solve our own vision problems. We might gladly accept the name and phone number of his eye doctor, but we would need an individual screening to determine corrective measures for our own vision. Yet we go to conferences and hear how someone built their church or ministry, and we expect to build ours the same way. It won't work!

Our loving heavenly Father is willing and able to show us our "vision from heaven." This is the plan and purpose for *our* lives that He has ordained — not our parents, not our teachers, or any other human being.

If you have not discovered your specific calling and mission, begin seeking the Holy Spirit's guidance today. Then always remember your uniqueness in Christ. Guard against distractions and detours. You are to accomplish God's will for your life, not someone else's!

PATIENCE

"Patience is accepting
a difficult situation
without giving God a
deadline to handle it."

*Be still before the Lord and
wait patiently for Him.*

Psalm 37:7

Have you ever prayed this prayer during an anxious moment, "Lord, give me patience...and I want it now!"

Have you ever taken a "crash course" on patience?

Do interruptions, inconveniences, and irritations test your patience?

Ministry is full of interruptions, inconveniences, and irritations — they come with the territory. The late night phone call after a car accident. A robbery at the church. A disgruntled parent in the middle of your sermon preparation. Irritable board members, irritable staff members, and board members who are irritated with staff members.

Sometimes it makes you want to change the words of "When We All Get to Heaven" to "When All *But You* Get to Heaven!"

The key to overcoming these trials is patience — a fruit of the Spirit. It is impossible to lead people without this Spirit-given virtue. Without it, the pulpit can become an artery of anger, the board agenda a strategy for revenge, and the preacher intolerant and ultimately unnecessary.

James 1:2,3 (KJV) says, "My brethren, count it all joy when ye fall into divers temptations; knowing *this*, that the trying of your faith worketh patience." Keep that in mind the next time trials of many kinds come your way —patience is being developed in you!

FAMILY

"Nowadays you'll find almost everything in the home — except the family."

He must manage his own family well and see that his children obey him with proper respect.

1 Timothy 3:4

An interesting *Newsweek* poll showed 49 percent of American fathers do a better job of parenting than their dads did. A majority of dads polled (54 percent) say they share equal parenting responsibilities with their wives, and 24 percent felt they do more than their spouses (51 percent of the mothers claim otherwise).

Whatever the figures, the real issue is how much we are involved in molding our children and grandchildren. Balancing family and ministry can be a difficult task, and the demands of the ministry can easily eclipse the needs of a minister's family.

Paul's admonition to ministers clearly teaches us that our *highest* calling is to take care of our families. To find that needed balance:

Make sure your children have fun at church.

Take a vacation!

Maintain *regular* office hours.

Go to your children's sporting events and activities.

Date your mate on a regular basis.

Make family altar time a priority.

Pray for your family daily.

Remember, your family is unique and God-given. Your first and foremost responsibilities of ministry are to them. They will be the greatest fulfillment and blessing in your life!

HONESTY

"Truth has only to exchange
hands a few times
to become fiction."

LORD, *who may dwell in your
sanctuary? Who may live on your
holy hill? He whose walk is blameless
and who does what is righteous,
who speaks the truth from his heart.*

Psalm 15:1,2

There's a story about three little boys who found a stray puppy. They were fussing over who would get the puppy and what to name the puppy.

They agreed that whoever could tell the biggest lie got to keep and name the puppy. A minister, overhearing the boys' plan, interrupted, "Boys, I'm disappointed in you. When I was your age, I *never* told a lie under *any* circumstance."

The boys looked at each other, handed the puppy to the preacher, and in unison said, "Reverend, whatcha gonna name your new puppy?"

A survey revealed that 66 percent of Americans feel it is not wrong to tell a lie. Only 31 percent agree that "Honesty is the best policy."

The integrity crisis that has infected this nation has prompted a movement of men called "Promise Keepers." Their focus is not only to be men of the Word, but men who keep their word.

As revealed in the story above, others know when we are not being truthful. As ministers of the truth, we must model truth, and being truthful 90 percent of the time is not integrity — it's hypocrisy!

Develop the *habit* of honesty and truthfulness in your life and your ministry. Being honest for the moment is oftentimes difficult, but being honest through the years brings peace and purity of heart.

INTEGRITY

"Integrity begins with how
I live when no one
is watching!"

*A GOOD name is better
than fine perfume.*

Ecclesiastes 7:1

Integrity is learned and demonstrated in many ways. One way we learn about personal integrity is when this boat we call "our life" is put into dry dock and fully exposed to what is above and below the water mark.

It is in these disruptive moments of life that we are most likely to display the integrity we possess. Integrity is almost tangible. Whenever we encounter it, we know we have found trust. It is utterly fascinating to see people who live by what might be called super-honesty, men and women who live at the "soul-level."

Alexander Whyte was one of those men. He was one of the great preaching heroes of 19th century Scotland. One day he was approached by a woman who showered him with words of praise. He knew the woman was sincere, but he also knew these kind words were not his to receive. In response to this lady's remarks, he said, "Madam, if you knew the man I really was, you would spit in my face."

Integrity begins with complete honesty at the fount of life — soul-level! Can you be considered by others to be living at that level of integrity? If you have any doubt, have the courage to let God search your heart and reveal the changes that need to be made. Then make those changes and watch your life become new!

JOY

"Joy is found in the presence of God."

*I have told you this so that
my joy may be in you and that
your joy may be complete.*

John 15:11

A gifted public speaker was asked to recall his most difficult speaking assignment. "That is easy," he answered. "It was an address I gave to the National Conference of Undertakers. The topic they gave me was, 'How to Look Sad at a Ten Thousand Dollar Funeral.'" Now that's a tough assignment!

But here's an assignment that can top that one: "How to Teach the Early Church to be Sad." The early believers had a joy that was unspeakable! It was unquenchable, unfathomable, and "unsquelchable."

Paul wrote from prison, "Rejoice in the Lord always. I will say it again: Rejoice" (Philippians 4:4). His joy was not dependent on his surroundings. His joy was dependent upon the Holy Spirit of God Who produces joy within.

Jesus is the joy of living;
He's the King of Life to me.
Unto Him my all I'm giving,
His forevermore to be.
I will do what He commands me;
Anywhere He leads I'll go.
Jesus is the joy of living;
He's the dearest friend I know.
— Alfred H. Ackley

Early Christians were filled with joy because Jesus gave them *hope* and *life*. Should we be any different?

FAILURE

"Failure is never final.
Staying down is!"

*There is not a righteous man on earth
who does what is right and never sins.*

Ecclcsiastes 7:20

Ted Williams was arguably one of the greatest hitters in the history of baseball. He was the last man to hit .400 and is now enshrined in the Baseball Hall of Fame. But Ted failed to get on base six out of every ten times he went to bat.

We often forget past successes and dwell on our past failures. We forget that failure is never final, and by doing so we allow failure to paralyze our ministry.

There are many things about our past that we would like to erase. Most of us, if it were possible, would change something in our personal histories. Would you like to take back a promise broken, a word spoken in anger, an action taken in haste, or a decision made unwisely?

Remember this: Failure is universal. James 3:2 reminds us that "we all stumble in many ways." Perhaps you are failing right now in some area of your life. But the key to getting past failure is to learn from it. Ask the Holy Spirit to show you where you went wrong and what was the root cause of your fall. Then work with Him to fix what needs to be fixed and go on.

It's also important to take a few moments and reflect on the fact that Jesus Christ loves you and believes in you despite your failures. See the exciting work He has for you. He has chosen you to spread His Word! And whenever you do stumble, He will pick you up, brush you off, and set you back on track — brighter and smarter than when you started!

VALUES

"Determine what is worth more and what is worth less than life and you'll find your core values."

Jim Williams

For where your treasure is, there your heart will be also.

Matthew 6:21

The Titanic was called the unsinkable ship, but it sank in the North Atlantic on the night of April 15, 1912. The ship rammed into an iceberg, which carved a 300-foot hole out of its hull. It disappeared into the dark waters within two and a half hours, and of the 2,200 passengers on board, only 705 survived.

A story is told of one man aboard the Titanic who, as the ship was sinking, offered another man a fistful of money in exchange for a seat in the life boat. The second man took the money and the first man took his seat. The man with the money never made it back alive.

One man valued money more than life; the other man valued life more than money. One man looked at the immediate; the other man looked at the long haul.

What and who do you live for?

What and who would you die for?

What is your first thought when you awake and your last thought before you sleep?

What are your dreams?

What is *your* treasure in life?

The answers to these questions will show you what your values are. Do you like them? If not, then change them!

REST

"To overcome stress,
enjoy a day off!"

*Jesus suggested, "Let's get away
from the crowds for a while
and rest." For so many people
were coming and going that
they scarcely had time to eat.*

Mark 6:31 TLB

God modeled rest for us at creation. He created the world in six days, then He rested on the seventh. Why? Was He tired? No! He simply wanted to teach us the importance of being refreshed by resting. If it's good enough for God, it's good enough for you and me!

Unfortunately, Sunday is not a day of rest for most of God's ministers. We are Sabbath breakers! (Today, we call them workaholics.)

It is interesting that in Psalm 23:2, the shepherd David writes, "He makes me lie down in green pastures." Have you ever had to make your children lie down? They get so wound up that you have to force them to rest. Yet we never make ourselves take a rest as an example to them.

Although you may take a regular day off during the week, you still feel required to tend the flock during that time. Sheep get sick on your day off. Lambs are born on your day off. Your family, friends, or an acquaintance you met only last week may hit a crisis and call for your counsel and prayer.

If you are burning the candle at both ends, you're not as bright as you think you are! Quit playing "Super-Minister" and delegate. Let a staff member or lay leader handle things on your day off. If we don't "come apart" as Jesus and His disciples did, eventually we will *come apart!*

MORALITY

"Learn as if you were to live forever; live as if you were to die tomorrow."

And do not grieve the Holy Spirit of God, with whom you were sealed for the day of redemption.

Ephesians 4:30

He was my mentor for preaching. As a young ministerial student I followed his ministry with great enthusiasm. He could sprinkle the stardust with his oratories. Without question, he will be remembered as one of the greatest campmeeting speakers of the 20th century.

Recently, my hero sat across the breakfast table from me. Having been removed from his pulpit, he was a broken man — a life in shambles and a ministry ruined by years of illicit sexual behavior that had finally caught up with him. At his age there was little hope for restoration to ministry.

As the tears flowed freely, my fallen preacher hero asked for my forgiveness. I reminded him that I loved and forgave him. I emphasized that God in heaven had also forgiven him. He acknowledged that he was forgiven through the shed blood of Jesus Christ.

As I watched him walk away, shoulders slumped, I thought of the mighty cleansing power of God's forgiveness and grace. I then thought of the people who might never hear one of his inspirational messages because of his sin. I still think he's the best ever to stand behind the sacred pulpit.

I know my hero is forgiven by God — just as you and I are. But the consequences of his sin are a grievous thing. We must never forget this any time we are tempted to disobey God's Word or the leading of the Holy Spirit.

COMMITMENT

"Stand for something or you'll fall for anything!"

For I am convinced that neither death nor life, neither angels nor demons, neither the present nor the future, nor any powers, neither height nor depth, nor anything else in all creation, will be able to separate us from the love of God that is in Christ Jesus our Lord.

Romans 8:38,39

The words of this African pastor have traveled millions of miles, reflecting the commitment level of God-ordained ministry.

"I'm part of the fellowship of the unashamed. I have Holy Spirit power. The die has been cast. I have stepped over the line. The decision has been made. I'm a disciple of His. I won't look back, let up, slow down, back away, or be still.

"My past is redeemed, my present makes sense, my future is secure. I'm finished and done with low living, sight walking, small planning, smooth knees, colorless dreams, tamed visions, mundane talking, cheap living, and dwarfed goals.

"I no longer need preeminence, prosperity, position, promotions, plaudits, or popularity. I don't have to be right, first, tops, recognized, praised, regarded, or rewarded. I now live by faith, lean on His presence, walk by patience, lift by prayer, and labor by power.

"I won't give up, shut up, let up, until I have stayed up, stored up, prayed up, paid up, preached up for the cause of Christ. I am a disciple of Jesus. I must go till He comes, give till I drop, preach till all know, and work till He stops me. And when He comes for His own, He will have no problem recognizing me — my banner will be clear!"

CALLING

"What you say is in God's name and for His sake."

Henry Blackaby

I press on toward the goal to win the prize for which God has called me heavenward in Christ Jesus.

Philippians 3:14

I had the opportunity to interview Dr. Henry Blackaby, author of *Experiencing God*,[6] for a future edition of P*astor to Pastor.* It was a powerful time as we talked about his life in Christ, his call to ministry, and his thoughts on ways folks like us can stay close to our Lord.

In his newest book, *The Power of the Call,* co-authored by Henry Brandt and Kerry Skinner, there is a defining quote about who you are, what you do, and why you do it. Blackaby writes: "You are the custodian of the most important information in the world. You are a specialist in what God has to say to people through the Bible. Your divine calling far supersedes all other professions. Your presence and impact have eternal consequences in the world. What you say is in God's name and for His sake."[7] That really puts a ribbon around your reason for being, doesn't it?

I am concerned that often people feel their contribution for the cause of Jesus Christ and to those they serve seems less than they had hoped. But never forget that the call of God on your life makes everything else pale in comparison! You have an awesome responsibility.

Philippians 1:6 says that God will complete the work He has begun in you. So remember what the Bible says and stay the course!

INFLUENCE

"Life is my college."

Louisa May Alcott

I thank God, whom I serve, as my forefathers did, with a clear conscience, as night and day I constantly remember you in my prayers.

2 Timothy 1:3

I am reminded of the men in my life upon whose shoulders I stand today.

There was a German professor who helped me through college. There was an unselfish, wise pastor who, when I was a 23-year-old rookie in his town, showed me the ropes. There was a near genius, though somewhat irreverent, clergyman who taught me to question the way of things — not to be obstinate — but just so I wouldn't miss something very important God was attempting to say to me.

There was my granddad who influenced me more than any other human being, because he loved me and believed in me when, in reality, I didn't deserve his confidence. And my dad who, though not a great father, loved me, and whom I admired because of his many gifts. I loved him and miss our times on the telephone. Then there is Jim Dobson, my cousin and very best friend, who offered me the chance to sculpt out a ministry for folks like you, providing an opportunity to lend some influence.

I have been influenced by so many wonderful leaders. I feel most blessed. How about you? Take a few moments to recall the men and women in your life who influenced you to be who you are today. Perhaps a note of thanks would be in order to those still alive. You may be surprised at the number of people who were there for you, unselfishly sowing into your life.

FAITH

"Change your thoughts and
change your world!"

Norman Vincent Peale

The apostles said to the Lord,
"Increase our faith!"

Luke 17:5

While speaking at a mission's conference in Orlando, Florida, I was greatly impressed with a small seven-year-old boy seated on the front row listening intently. I had a flashback to the hills of West Virginia where I grew up, for it was at age seven that I received my call to preach the Gospel while seated on the front row of a service.

I watched the young boy as he responded to his pastor's invitation to fill out a faith promise and commit to give on a systematic basis to the cause of world evangelism. Little did I know that he had pledged a grand total of $20!

As I prepared to leave the conference and go to the airport I felt strangely impressed to give his grandfather a humorous book I had written. I carefully signed the book, placed a $20 bill inside, and gave it to his grandfather to give to him. I really wasn't sure why I did it — I just felt it!

At the evening service, the grandfather gave the book to the little boy, not knowing that I had placed the $20 bill inside the cover. Moments later, believing that God had placed the money in my book for him, the boy joyfully proclaimed that God had performed a miracle, promptly paid his pledge, and shared his miracle of faith with the other believers.

And it was a miracle! Even if I had not placed the $20 in the book, God would have provided it for him. How do I know? Because God honors the faith of a little child!

TIME

"In primitive societies no one
has a watch, but everyone has
time. In advanced societies,
everyone has a watch,
but no one has any time."

Gerhard Geschwandtner

Teach us to number our days aright,
that we may gain a heart of wisdom

Psalm 90:12

Most ministers I know feel like they don't have enough time each day to do all the things they are expected to do. At a time management seminar, the speaker pointed out how the average person will waste many hours in the span of a normal life:

Opening junk mail: 8 months.

Sitting at stoplights: 6 months.

Searching for misplaced objects: 1 year.

Trying to return phone calls to people who never seem to be in: 2 years.

Standing in line: 5 years.

After hearing the speaker, I have tried to use the following to manage my time well: The test of necessity, appropriateness, and efficiency.

Ralph Waldo Emerson once said, "One of the illusions of life is that the present hour is not the critical, decisive hour. Write it on your heart that every day is the best day of the year." Taking a cue from Emerson, we would probably get more accomplished by realizing that every minute represents an eternal investment of our lives and the lives of others.

Do "time thieves" pop up throughout your day? Ask God to show you during what times of the day you are most likely to succumb to these thieves. Value each moment as a gift from the Lord.

DREAMS

"We grow by dreams."

Woodrow Wilson

*Nobody should seek his own good,
but the good of others.*

1 Corinthians 10:24

On the final page of the book, *The Heart of a Great Pastor,* there is a quote from an anonymous writer who offers hope to those who have suffered the agony of broken hearts, hopes, and dreams. "We've dreamed many dreams that never came true. We've seen them vanish at dawn. But we've realized enough of our dreams, thank God, to make us want to dream on."[8]

As I have observed the life and ministry of my colleagues through the years, it has always been those who refuse to allow the "dream" to leave them that seem to press on in spite of the challenges they face. I think the reason they are able to do this so successfully is because they honestly believe their dreams are the work of the Holy Spirit. As impossible as they may appear, these dreams are authored by our loving Lord.

For most of us, the size of our faith influences the size of our dreams, but the thing I fear most for you is that you will look at the difficulty of your assignment, grow calloused, simply throw up your hands, and say, "Who cares? What's the use?"

God cares! And He has called you to "dream the impossible dream" with Him. The Bible says that if we delight ourselves in the Lord, He will give us the desires of our hearts. (See Psalm 37:4.) Isn't that what dreams are — the desires He has placed in our hearts? Dare to dream big and watch God fulfill that dream in you.

TEMPTATION

"Character is like a tree and
reputation like its shadow. Th
shadow is what we think of it
the tree is the real thing."

Abraham Lincoln

*No temptation has seized you
except what is common to man.
And God is faithful; he will not
let you be tempted beyond what
you can bear. But when you are
tempted, he will also provide a way ou
so that you can stand up under it.*

1 Corinthians 10:13

An article in *Enrichment* magazine asked the question, "When are you most likely to face temptation?" Respondents were allowed multiple choices. Of those surveyed,

- 81 percent said it was when they had not spent much time with God;
- 57 percent when they had not had enough rest;
- 45 percent when life was difficult;
- 42 percent during times of change; and
- 37 percent after a significant spiritual victory.

These figures profiled a substantial number of ministers I meet along the way. Unfortunately, I recently heard of two more of our colleagues who yielded to temptation and failed morally.

I remind you to "flee the evil desires of youth, and pursue righteousness, faith, love and peace, along with those who call on the Lord out of a pure heart" (2 Timothy 2:22). Read the list above again and see if these do not represent your danger zones.

There is a "new wind" blowing amidst the Church and Satan is doing all he can to prevent the Spirit's outpouring. Let us not be guilty of "putting out the Spirit's fire" through our own moral weakness.

Remember the admonition of Paul to the Corinthians: There is not one temptation coming your way that God has not already provided a way of escape — so escape!

NEGATIVISM

"Everything can be taken from a man but one thing: the last o the human freedoms — to choose one's attitude in any given set of circumstances."

Victor E. Frankl

Finally, brothers, whatever is true, whatever is noble, whatever is right, whatever is pure, whatever is lovely, whatever is admirable — if anything is excellent or praiseworthy — think about such things.

Philippians 4:8

In my book, *Your Pastor Is An Endangered Species — A Wake-Up Call to the Local Church*, I spend a chapter discussing the mindset that kept the children of Israel in the desert for 40 additional years. Caleb, a faith-filled visionary, said, "Let's possess the land," but the negative ones "spread...a bad report about the land they had explored" (Numbers 13:30,32).[9]

As I talk with ministers and church leaders across the country, I hear of clergy and laymen alike who, because of a negative, complaining attitude, spread a contagious spirit that keeps churches in the desert for years. A negative spirit is like a deadly pollutant. Though it harms everyone, it usually hurts the one who expresses it the most.

For the children of Israel, the consequences were many. They grumbled about how dangerous it was to go into the promised land without giving thought to how dangerous it was to stay outside of it.

They missed God's promise because of a negative spirit rooted in the irrational fears of unbelief. (See Hebrews 4:6.) They forgot that, even though the "giants" were large, their God promised to be larger.

Isn't it often similar with Christians today? Agree with Paul: "If anything is excellent or praiseworthy — think about such things." Be a visionary, shun all negativism, think and speak only good things, and possess the land!

MIRACLES

"There is no hope
but in prayer."

Andrew Bonar

*"If you can?" said Jesus. "Everything
is possible for him who believes."*

Mark 9:23

In my book, *God's Never Failed Me, But He's Sure Scared Me To Death A Few Times*, there's a story about two nuns who were delivering medical supplies to a nursing home when their car ran out of gas. They searched the car for a gas can, but could only find a bedpan. The sisters walked a half a mile to a gas station and filled the bedpan with gas.

Upon returning to their car, they carefully balanced the bedpan and began to pour the gas into the tank. About that time a man driving a pickup truck approached. When he saw what was going on, he came to a complete stop. Marveling at what he thought he was seeing, he stuck his head out of the truck window and said, "Sisters, I'm not Catholic, but I'll tell you what. I sure do admire your faith!"[10]

Most people admire ministers for their faith and depend on them for their prayers, especially prayers that call for miraculous results. I want to live in a way that people will do more than admire my faith. I want to live so close to God that they will have the confidence to ask me to pray for them to receive a miracle!

Are you in need of a miracle? You serve a miracle-working God! He wants to work miracles in and through your life.

FRIENDSHIP

"The only way to have
a friend is to be one."

Anonymous

*A man of many companions
may come to ruin, but there is a
friend who sticks closer than a brother*

Proverbs 18:24

I have never enjoyed long vacations, because the longer I'm away, the more I think about church, home, etc. Several years ago I learned to take crisp, brief vacations. I've found they relax me more than the "monster" trips. I love "mini" vacations!

One weekend my wife and I met "old" friends from college days in New York City and attended a Broadway play. It was so much fun! We hated to say goodbye. As we were leaving for the airport, my college quartet buddy and roommate gave me a hug and said, "Old friends are the greatest friends!" I hastily wiped a tear from my eye and thought, "I'm too young to be this sentimental!"

My wife often says, "You're everyone's friend!" That could very well be true. I love people, and as a minister I've run every stop sign and have spent a great deal of time becoming friends with my parishoners. However, I have no regrets about being vulnerable enough to develop lasting friendships. It has paid huge dividends in terms of my ministry.

Today, there's lots of talk about "networking." Personally, I would like to see church leaders focus on friendship-building. Whether you are a pastor or a traveling minister, a missionary or a volunteer church member, be a good friend to those God entrusts to you as family, associates, and "bosom buddies." Remember, Jesus said the world would know us by the way we love one another! (See John 13:35.)

LEGACY

"The great use of life is
to spend it for something
that outlasts it."

William James

So then, brothers, stand firm and hol
to the teachings we passed on to you,
whether by word of mouth or by letter

2 Thessalonians 2:15

When the historical Nashville First Church of the Nazarene celebrated 100 years serving the heart of the city, I was among the four former pastors interviewed. Each of us was asked, "What would you like to be remembered for during your pastoral service at this great church?"

Carefully, I responded, "...that I loved God, loved my family, and loved the people greatly." Until that moment, I really hadn't thought much about the "legacy" I left that church.

How will we be remembered? I believe we will be remembered for the words we speak, the actions we take, the love we give, and the cards and letters we write.

Talk show host Larry King reported that during a hospital stay he received many letters and gifts. However, the one which touched him the most was a Bible and note sent by Pete Maravich, former NBA star. The note read: "Dear Larry, I'm so glad to hear that everything went well with your surgery. I want you to know that God was watching over you every minute, and even though I know you may question that, I also know that one day it will be revealed to you...because He lives."

The following week, Pete Maravich died. He will always be remembered by Larry King as a *caring* Christian.

How will you be remembered? If you are not satisfied with your answer, it's never too late to change it. Ask yourself how you want your family, friends, church, and associates to remember you — and then go make the memories!

LOVE

"If we do not show love to one another, the world has a right to question whether Christianity is true."

Francis A. Schaeffer

Love the Lord your God with all your heart and with all your soul and with all your mind. This is the first and greatest commandment. And the second is like it: Love your neighbor as yourself.

Matthew 22:37-39

THE **MINISTER'S** LITTLE DEVOTIONAL BOOK

Complete this sentence: My greatest aim in life is....

How you respond determines the guiding principle of your life.

God's greatest aim for your life and ministry is love. Without love, all that you say is ineffective, all that you know is incomplete, all that you believe is insufficient, all that you give is inadequate, and all that you accomplish is insignificant.

LIFE MINUS LOVE = NOTHING

Christianity is not a religion of beliefs — it is a lifestyle of love. The sign of a true Christian is not a crucifix, a fish, or a bumper sticker. The sign of a true Christian is their love for God and for His people. Galatians 5:6 says, "The only thing that counts is faith expressing itself through love."

An enemy of love is "busyness." Clear the clutter of your schedule and let love be the order of the day. More than video games, trampolines, and the latest novelty toy, children need love. More than a new pair of shoes or a new dress, wives need love. More than a new set of golf clubs or a fishing pole, husbands need love.

For Christians, love is not an option, it is a commandment — sometimes difficult to obey. But God did not leave you helpless, "...because the love of God is shed abroad in our hearts by the Holy Ghost" (Romans 5:5 KJV). Draw upon God's love for you to love the "unlovable."

PEACE

"Peace is not the absence of problems. Peace is the presence of God."

Thou wilt keep him in perfect peace, whose mind is stayed on thee: because he trusteth in thee.

Isaiah 26:3 KJV

When the storms of life come (and they will come) we can be filled with panic, or we can be filled with peace. Peace is not the absence of problems.

How can we experience peace in the *midst* of life's storms? First of all, we must remember God is right there with us. "Fear not, for I have redeemed you; I have summoned you by name; you are mine. When you pass through the waters, I will be with you; and when you pass through the rivers, they will not sweep over you. When you walk through the fire, you will not be burned; the flames will not set you ablaze" (Isaiah 43:1,2).

The second thing we must do to experience God's peace is to relax in His care. First Peter 5:7 says, "Cast all your anxiety on him because he cares for you."

Finally, to experience God's peace we must rely on His control. When things get out of control, we get anxious. The good news is that the things that are beyond our control are not beyond God's control. Jeremiah 32:17 says, "Ah, Sovereign Lord, you have made the heavens and the earth by your great power and outstretched arm. Nothing is too hard for you."

What is robbing you of peace today? Make this familiar chorus the prayer of your heart:

> Peace! Peace! Wonderful peace, Coming down from the Father above! Sweep over my spirit forever, I pray, In fathomless billows of love.

"Wonderful Peace," by W. D. Cornell[11]

GENTLENESS

"You can walk hand-in-hand without seeing eye-to-eye."

Let your gentleness be evident to all.

Philippians 4:5

If you want to be liked (and who doesn't?) it helps to be likable. One of the most likable qualities a minister can possess is gentleness. To be gentle means to be understanding, not demanding.

Interestingly enough, only two people in the Bible were referred to as being gentle — Jesus and Moses.

Proverbs 4:7 says, "Though it cost all you have, get understanding." Understanding works everywhere — at home, at the office, in a board meeting, even in traffic. God puts up with a lot from us, probably because He understands us. And if God can tolerate our inconsistencies and shortcomings, we must learn to understand one another. This is gentleness.

"Gentleness" is sometimes translated "meekness." We mistakenly tend to equate "meekness" with "weakness." Like the domineering wife who said to her husband, "What are you, man or mouse? Go ahead, squeak up!" The meek, the gentle, whose strength is controlled by the Holy Spirit, are God's kind of people. Jesus said in the Beatitudes, "They will inherit the earth" (Matthew 5:5).

If you want to live a lonely, unfulfilling life: Never admit you are wrong. Know it all. Always talk, never listen.

It is true, you will never see eye-to-eye with everybody all the time. But gentleness, which is the fruit of the Spirit, can help you walk hand-in-hand.

LISTENING

"It's all right to hold a conversation as long as you let go of it once in a while."

My dear brothers, take note of this:
Everyone should be quick to listen,
slow to speak and slow
to become angry.

James 1:19

A man joined a monastery to become a monk. Each year, the young monk was permitted to speak only two words. The first year he said, "Food cold." After another year of silence, he said, "Bed hard." After year three he said, "I quit!"

His superior said, "I'm not surprised — all you've done since you've been here is complain!"

Six words in three years is tough for the average American. We spend one-fifth of our lives talking. We engage in 30 conversations per day. We speak 20,000-30,000 words per day.

Every Sunday millions of people go to church and hear billions of words in sermons. And when it's all said and done, more will be said than done.

James exhorts, "...be quick to listen, slow to speak." The good Lord gave us two ears and one tongue. Do you suppose He intended for us to listen twice as much as we speak?

As Christians, our first responsibility is to listen to the Holy Spirit. Galatians 5:16 tells us, "So I say, live by the Spirit, and you will not gratify the desires of the sinful nature."

Have you heard from the Holy Spirit today? Some of us just need to stop, stand still, and be quiet long enough to hear Him when we are engaged in conversation or called upon to speak. Sometimes, only listening to Him can keep us from putting our foot in our mouth!

HEALING

"I heard about His healing, of His cleansing pow'r revealing. How He made the lame to walk again and caused the blind to see. And then I cried, 'Dear Jesus,come and heal my broken spirit.'And somehow Jesus came and brought to me the victory."

"Victory in Jesus"
by Eugene M. Bartlett

He said to her, "Daughter, your faith has healed you. Go in peace and be freed from your suffering."

Mark 5:34

As Jesus was on His way to help the daughter of Jairus, a large crowd followed Him. In the crowd that day was a woman who had been ill for 12 years. She wasn't like the rest of the crowd, however. They were following Jesus to see what He was going to do for *someone else,* but she was following Jesus to see what He was going to do for *her!*

As ministers, we're sometimes like the crowd following Jesus. We are interested in what He can do for others, but rarely come to Him for ourselves. It almost takes a desperate situation before we "approach the throne of grace with confidence, so that we may receive mercy and find grace to help us in our time of need" (Hebrews 4:16).

Perhaps you have been ill or have suffered many years physically, financially, or emotionally. Why not exercise your faith for yourself? Reach out and touch the hem of His garment just like the woman in Mark, chapter 5.

Do not limit what God can do for you because of your lack of faith, either. F. B. Meyer said, "Unbelief puts our circumstances between us and God. Faith puts God between us and our circumstances."

Do not allow your faith to become comfortable and complacent. Stretch your faith! Open your heart to Jesus today, and give Him the opportunity to say to you, "Your faith has healed you. Go in peace and be freed from your suffering."

LAMENTATIONS

"When the whole world stinks, the problem is probably right under your nose."

The Lord is like an enemy...
He has multiplied mourning
and lamentation.

Lamentations 2:5

The town drunk was passed out on the sidewalk. Some kids thought they would play a trick on him by rubbing some aged cheese under his nose. When he awoke, the aroma caused him to say, "This neighborhood stinks." He pulled himself up and caught a bus. Stepping on the bus he said, "This bus stinks!" Getting off the bus on the other side of town he said, "This neighborhood stinks too!"

When the whole world stinks, the problem is probably right under our nose. As ministers, we sometimes make some common mistakes: Instead of accentuating the positive, we exaggerate the negative. We allow facts to be replaced by feelings. We compare our ministry to another's ministry. And we blame ourselves for things that aren't our fault.

Common mistakes are blown way out of proportion, one little thing on top of another, until finally we hear ourselves lamenting, "The Lord is like an enemy...He has multiplied mourning and lamentation."

At times like these, there is only one remedy: prayer. *Father, forgive me for becoming more conscious of my problems than I am of You! Now, as I live my life in harmony with You, help me not to lose the focus of my ministry. Replace stress with Your strength, replace my burdens with Your blessing, and replace my pain with Your peace. Thank You so much, in Jesus name. Amen.*

DEPRESSION

"Sally says to Charlie Brown,
'We have to write a short piece
for school that expresses
our personal philosophy.
So far I've written, *Who cares?*
and *Forget it.*'

Charlie Brown says,
'How about, *Why me?*'

Sally says, 'That's good,
I'll fit it in.'"

*But O my soul, don't be discouraged.
Don't be upset. Expect God to act! For
know that I shall again have plenty of
reason to praise him for all that he will
do. He is my help! He is my God!*

Psalm 42:11 TLB

Depression is not a new problem for God's ministers. Moses, Elijah, and Jonah became so depressed that they asked God to take their lives. David talked candidly about his depression in Psalm 42.

Depression is usually a symptom of another problem. Sometimes ministers simply get weary in well-doing. That is what happened to Moses. God told Moses to delegate. "I will take of the Spirit that is on you and put the Spirit on them. They will help you carry the burden of the people so that you will not have to carry it alone" (Numbers 11:17).

Fatigue, frustration, fear, and failure can quickly move God's ministers from the highs of Mount Carmel to the lows of a broom tree. When depression overtakes you, consider these action steps:

1. Take a break.
2. Get some exercise.
3. Delegate.
4. Don't expect too much of yourself.
5. See your physician.
6. Talk to the "Great Physician."

FORGIVENESS

"A sign at the entrance
of a convent read,

Absolutely NO TRESPASSING!

Violators will be prosecuted
to the full extent of the law.

Signed, The Sisters of Mercy"

*For if you forgive men when they
sin against you, your heavenly
Father will also forgive you.*

Matthew 6:14

A four-year-old got confused praying the Lord's Prayer. He prayed, "And forgive us our trash baskets as we forgive those who put trash in our baskets."

That's pretty much what Jesus meant by His words in Matthew 6:14. Jesus went on to say in verse 15, "But if you do not forgive men their sins, your Father will not forgive your sins."

The church is simply a community of forgiven and forgiving sinners. Every individual who attends church on Sunday morning has fallen short of the glory of God. Some, however, have received God's free gift of salvation by grace!

Because God has forgiven you, you must forgive others. Why? Is this just another commandment "for your own good?" Yes!

Bitterness, anger, or a critical attitude will bring sickness to your heart and eventually to your body. Forgiveness will make you free and release the Holy Spirit to bring healing to your life.

So give up your grudges, grief, and guilt. Empty your trash basket today!

Ephesians 4:31,32 GNB says, "Get rid of all bitterness, passion, and anger. No more shouting or insults, no more hateful feelings of any sort. Instead, be kind and tenderhearted to one another, and forgive one another, as God has forgiven you through Christ."

LAUGHTER

"If you're not allowed to laugh in heaven, I don't want to go there."

Martin Luther

Sarah said, "God has brought me laughter, and everyone who hears about this will laugh with me."

Genesis 21:6

The word *laugh* first appears in Genesis 17:17, when God told 100-year-old Abraham that his 90-year-old wife Sarah was going to have a baby. The Bible says Abraham fell on his face and laughed.

Later in chapter 18, three visitors (the Lord among them) appear and tell Abraham again that he and Sarah will have a son. Sarah is eavesdropping, and when she hears she is to have a baby she also laughs. In chapter 21 the child is born, and Abraham names him Isaac, which means "God's laugh."[12]

God really does have a sense of humor. Seminary won't teach that in systematic theology, but take it from Abraham and Sarah — God has a sense of humor!

In my mind, I can picture Saturday nights in heaven. All the preachers are sitting around God's throne telling their best Sunday morning pulpit bloopers. Don't tell me God doesn't laugh — He made preachers!

When was the last time you had a really good laugh? It's scriptural, you know — even theraputic. Proverbs 17:22 KJV says, "A merry heart doeth good like a medicine."

A Prayer for Laughter

Lord, help me today to create more laughter than tears. People look better and feel better when they laugh. Let me be a dispenser of joy and fun. Never allow me to forget that ministry is all about encouragement. Amen.

MODERNITY

"I can do what you can't do, and you can do what I can't do. Together we can do great things."

Mother Teresa

But you will receive power when the Holy Spirit comes on you.

Acts 1:8

Reading through the book, *More Than Conquerors — Portraits of Believers from All Walks of Life,* I ran across a statement made by the late great preacher and author, A. W. Tozer. He writes, "Save me from the curse that lies across the face of the modern clergy, the curse of compromise, of imitation, and of professionalism. Save me from the error of judging a church by its size, its popularity or the amount of its yearly offering. Help me to remember that I am a prophet; not a promoter, not a religious manager."[13]

Dr. Tozer died in 1963 with a reputation as one who did not pull punches. He spoke the truth.

Reflecting on Tozer's comments, I am also reminded of Os Guinness' term *modernity* — the spirit, system, and sum total of everything that makes up our modern world.

Al McDonald once said, "Modern management can be the kiss of death if it overshadows rather than reinforces the basic mission of the church. Without care we might settle for something that looks genuine, but is not!"

Modernity can function as a substitute for the Holy Spirit if we are not careful. For example, if things are going well, we can operate in our power for long periods of time without even noticing He's missing! That concerns me. How about you? We would all do well to take a good, long, prayerful look at our ministries and ask the Holy Spirit to show us where modernity has usurped Him.

PURITY

"Always counsel with
the door open!"

Stan Toler

*But among you there must not be
even a hint of sexual immorality,
or of any kind of impurity.*

Ephesians 5:3

With the talk about immorality among our political leaders, it is appropriate to address the subject of moral purity.

Scarcely a day goes by in our Pastoral Ministries offices that we don't hear from a clergy person who has jeopardized his or her ministry due to moral failure.

The more we talk to our colleagues, the clearer it becomes that, beyond the sin issue, these situations result from one being burned out, careless in counseling, or unwilling to resolve issues of weakness or problems within their marriage.

In Peter Wagner's book, *Prayer Shield*, he lists several very wise suggestions and safeguards for our consideration:

1. Do not visit with a member of the opposite sex alone at home.
2. Do not discuss detailed sexual problems with the opposite sex in counseling.
3. Do not discuss your own marriage problems with an attender of the opposite sex.
4. Be careful in answering cards and letters from the opposite sex.
5. Do not show questionable affection to the opposite sex.[14]

In light of the warning from the apostle Paul, these words are very timely. Please implement this list if you haven't already. Do not give the enemy the slightest foothold!

SUPPORT

"As the yellow gold is tried in
fire, so the faith of friendship
must be seen in adversity."

Ovid

*Lead me, O Lord, in your
righteousness because of my enemies –
make straight your way before me.*

Psalm 5:8

I have received many letters from ministers' spouses who are very concerned about you, their mates. They write about your anxieties, the number of hours you put in each week, and how fatigued you seem. They write about your time at home — when your body is with them, but your mind is elsewhere.

They write about the financial pressures you carry, both for the ministry and the home, and how frustrated you get when there is just no more to go around. They write that they wish you had a close friend with whom you could be open and honest.

So often they fear that you feel they don't really understand. They get frustrated when they see you taking heat from contentious believers who care more about themselves than they do the body of Christ. They worry about your kids and how the children deal internally with what they see and hear.

But do you know what they write about most?

They talk about how much they love you, how proud they are of you, and how often they pray for you.

You are blessed, my friend!

Why not resolve to let your spouse know regularly how much their support and prayers mean to you?

SEARCHING

"God will never lead
you where His strength
cannot keep you."

Anonymous

Dear children, let us not love
with words or tongue but
with actions and in truth.

1 John 3:18

Some of you will remember the 1980 country-western hit by Johnny Lee, "Looking for Love," but the words may have escaped you:

Looking for love in all the wrong places.

Looking for love in too many faces.

Searching for hearts, looking for traces of what I'm dreaming of....

Why the song, you say? Because I see a tie-in to the 39 cult members who committed suicide in early 1997 near San Diego, California. They also were looking for love and acceptance. They were looking for a significance that had escaped them, and in so doing they encountered people looking for the same thing.

Now that I've found a friend and a lover,

I bless the day I discovered another heart — looking for love.[15]

There are so many folks who come and go from your ministry who are looking for a place to belong — a connection with people that will be authentic and genuine. I wonder if we are not spending so much time attempting to influence the masses of people that we overlook the nameless, faceless attenders who will give a church "a little while" to love them, and if it doesn't, go looking for love in all the wrong places.

Please do not overlook those who are searching. Introduce them to the only true and lasting love of Jesus by showing them His love yourself.

COMPARING YOURSELF

"Most people are willing
to take the Sermon on the
Mount as a flag to sail under,
but few will use it as a rudder
by which to steer."

Oliver Wendell Holmes

*We do not dare to classify
or compare ourselves with
some who commend themselves.
When they measure themselves by
themselves and compare themselves
with themselves, they are not wise.*

2 Corinthians 10:12

It happens every day. We turn on the television and see a well-dressed, silver-tongued orator who can preach circles around us. Incensed, and even a bit green with envy, we drive down the street and can't help but see that Dr. Smell Fungus has Mega in front of his church name.

Aristotle reminded the world that excellence was not an act, but rather a habit. If this is true, then we must ask the question, "How do I measure up?"

Cathy Rigby was the hope of the United States at the 1972 Olympic games in Munich, Germany. She had one goal in mind — excellence! Before the games began, she prayed for strength to move her through the routine without making a mistake.

She performed well, but she did not win. Emotionally, she was crushed. She joined her parents in the stands, ready for a good cry. "I'm sorry", she said, "I did my best."

Today, Cathy recalls ten words from her mother that she will never forget. "Doing *your* best is more important than being *the* best."

The adage is still true — do your best and leave the rest to the Father. You have enough challenges in ministry without beating yourself up because another minister does something well. Your personal levels of excellence are found in your relationship with the Holy Spirit. He will let you know when you have done your best and when you held back.

SPEECH

"He who reigns within himself and rules his passions, desires, and fears is more than a king."

For where you have envy and selfish ambition, there you find disorder and every evil practice.

James 3:16

We were able to see a perfect example of the old adage, "Loose lips sink ships," and its subsequent consequences when Fuzzy Zoeller, a veteran of the PGA golf tour, made an off-handed remark about one of his younger colleagues, Tiger Woods. He referred to Tiger as "that little boy" and urged him not to request fried chicken and collard greens for the champion's dinner at next year's Masters. His remarks cost him his endorsements with K-Mart and participation in a tournament in the Carolinas.

We in the clergy can be some of the worst offenders when it comes to idle gossip about one another. I must plead guilty myself! It seems we are intrigued by the misfortune of others in our ranks and spend an inordinate amount of time talking to one another about it. The Zoeller/Woods incident reminded me of how careful we must be when we discuss the life and ministry of one of our own.

Paul wrote in Ephesians 4:29, "Do not let any unwholesome talk come out of your mouths, but only what is helpful for building others up...." I not only say amen to that, but I also pray, "Oh Lord, please help me keep my mouth shut!"

Zoeller issued an apology, and perhaps that might be fitting for many of us. Some of us need to apologize and some of us need to forgive those who have spoken ill of us. Every human being is tempted to talk of the faults and weaknesses of others — especially those they envy or dislike. But ministers ought to set the standard of godly speech.

AUTHORITY

"It's hard, in a few minutes
on Sunday morning, to
offset the values presented
through the media in
the course of the week."

William Keeler
National Conference of
Catholic Bishops

*WHEN JESUS had called the
Twelve together, he gave them
power and authority to drive out
all demons and to cure diseases.*

Luke 9:1

As I think about the Easter season, I am reminded of a conversation Jesus had with His disciples. They were troubled over his words, "In a little while you will see me no more" (John 16:17).

To help them better understand, He comforted them by saying, "You will grieve, but your grief will turn to joy...and no one will take away your joy" (vv. 20,22).

It was Jesus' sacrifice that would constitute both sorrow and joy for them. And it was in the name of the risen Christ — Jesus — that they would find the power and authority to do the work of ministry after Jesus ascended into heaven.

It is the same with you. Your authority, your power, and your credibility do not come because you are talented, gifted, charming, or articulate — but through the name of the Lord Jesus Christ.

The church can be full of itself, parading its organization and programs before the world. At times, it is even boastful in its accomplishments. But be reminded of the words Jesus spoke in John 15:5, "Apart from me you can do nothing."

I wonder what it will take before we fully catch on to His admonition. He is risen! And that means that with Him, we can accomplish everything He has called us to do and be all He has ordained us to be.

REGRETS

"From the errors of others,
a wise man corrects his own."

Syrus

*Therefore, I urge you, brothers,
in view of God's mercy, to offer
your bodies as living sacrifices,
holy and pleasing to God — this
is your spiritual act of worship.*

Romans 12:1

In the October 20, 1996, issue of *Parade* magazine, Dr. Billy Graham was asked by reporter Colin Greer, "How would you most like to be remembered?" Graham paused for a moment, then said, "That I was faithful to do what God wanted me to do. That I maintained integrity in every area of my life, and that I lived what I preached."

When asked if he had any regrets, Graham replied, "I would have spent more time with each of my children. Also, I would have studied more."

As I read his words, it occurred to me that this man, friend of presidents and preacher to more than 200 million people in live audience settings, is not really much different in his wants and regrets than most of us.

For Dr. Graham, the journey is nearing an end, but for many of us, there is time to make the changes we know we need to make.

Here are some questions to ask yourself today:

1. How much time do I spend each day with my kids?

2. Am I careless in matters of morality and integrity?

3. Do I practice what I preach?

4. Do I have any regrets?

In order to finish well and have few regrets, we must daily evaluate every aspect of our lives.

PURPOSE

"All great men and women became great because they invested time, talent, and ability in the care of others."

From him the whole body, joined and held together by every supporting ligament, grows and builds itself up in love, as each part does its work.

Ephesians 4:16

I thought the great snowstorm the country experienced one winter had finally caught up with me when my flight to Memphis was delayed for quite some time. However, I learned it was not due to the weather, but rather because one flight attendant was absent.

Evidently, the plane could not operate without three attendants, and there were only two. So we waited and waited. When the missing employee was finally located, the boarding crew broke out into wild applause. Just think — the entire flight operation of the airline, hundreds of passengers, and a multi-million dollar aircraft were all grounded because of one person.

In many ways, your position as a minister can have that same kind of impact on the world you serve. At times it may seem as though your presence is scarcely noticed. But consider what the lives of many individuals and families might be like if you were not there to offer counsel, direction, and even caution; to listen and pray; and to let them know they are loved and valued.

The classic Christmas movie, "It's A Wonderful Life," gives one of the finest illustrations of how each one of us has a tremendous purpose to fulfill, a purpose that is vital to those we love as well as those we may never meet. I call this the "ministry of presence" — just being at the right place at the right time.

Always remember: You really do matter!

DEVOTION

"Men will get no more
out of life than what
they put into it."

William Boetcker

*They devoted themselves to the apostles
teaching and to the fellowship, to the
breaking of bread and to prayer.*

Acts 2:42

My mother often shared a story in children's church that beautifully illustrates what happens when we are truly devoted to a cause or mission.

A little boy had been taught by his father how to carve toys out of wood. As a result of his father's influence, the young boy became devoted to the mission of carving a complete boat. He built one complete with sails, rigging, and rudder.

The day came for the boy to test his wooden vessel for its sea worthiness. He carefully placed his boat into the nearby lake and watched it drift farther into the large body of water. Suddenly, a gust of wind grabbed the boat and broke the twine that was attached to the vessel. Tearfully, he watched his prize possession sail out of sight.

Devoted to the mission of recovering his boat, the young boy visited stores that sold toy boats. One day he found his boat and purchased it back from the shop owner. His mission was finally fufilled!

Ministry demands that kind of devotion.

Do you seek after the lost with the same fervency the little boy sought after his boat?

Are you completely committed to doing all you can for the kingdom of God, knowing that the end result is your mission fulfilled?

AFFECTION

"Acceptance is the truest kinship with humanity."

G. K. Chesterton

Be devoted to one another in brotherly love.

Romans 12:10

A Sunday school teacher once asked a large group of adults, "Does anyone need a hug?" How thoughtful! Everyone needs a hug!

Quite often when I counsel young couples approaching their wedding day, I ask the question, "How were feelings of love expressed in your respective homes while growing up?" Many times they will respond, "We hugged. We said, 'I love you.'"

It is critical for those in ministry to experience warmth and affection with their families and fellow Christians. But unfortunately, it is the missing link in many church parsonages. Many spouses confide, they just don't feel loved!

Morris Weigelt often shares about a time he experienced deep depression. Once, I heard him talk about his hospitalization. He said, "It was very late at night and all of my insecurities and depression overwhelmed me. I got out of bed and walked the halls of the hospital looking for someone who was awake and willing to hug me."

With a great deal of pathos and humor, he concluded that all he could find was a huge, burly security guard. "Sir, will you give me a hug?" he asked.

"I sure will!" the security guard responded. Dr. Weigelt indicated that in that affectionate hug, he found comfort and encouragement. He was able to return to his room and sleep peacefully.

Ministers, hug your family today!

BUSYNESS

"You must do the very thing you cannot do."

Eleanor Roosevelt

From the Lord comes deliverance.
May your blessing be on your people.

Psalm 3:8

Do you know the story of the father who loved his son very much, but couldn't find the time to give him attention?

The son wanted to build a tree house, but the father always seemed to have an excuse that precluded him from doing so. One day, after a serious accident, the son lay dying in the hospital. The dad was frantic to relate to his son and save his life, but as the boy's condition worsened, he knew it was hopeless.

The last words the father heard from his son were, "I'm sorry, Dad, it looks like we won't get around to building that tree house after all." How painful that must have been.

I was guilty of getting caught up in the fast-paced schedule of pastoring, often at the expense of those I loved. So, what would I do differently if I had another chance?

I would act on, not talk about, how much I loved my family. Each week, I would share a quality event with my boys. I would have a date every week — no matter what — with my wife.

I would honor my family by taking a day off each week. I would not burden them so much with the challenges I faced, and I would proclaim by my actions how valuable they were to me.

Does your family know without a doubt that they are more important to you than *anything*? I pray so! But if not, ask God to show you how to make things right.

BASICS

"Clergy persons have
abandoned the basics."

Eugene Peterson

*KEEP ME safe, O God,
for in you I take refuge.*

Psalm 16:1

A chapter in Eugene Peterson's book, *Working the Angles,* says some very interesting, but troubling things about pastors: "I don't know of any other profession in which it is quite as easy to fake it as in ours. [We can do so] by adopting a reverential demeanor, cultivating a stained-glass voice, slipping occasional words like 'eschatology' into conversation — not often enough to confuse people, but enough to keep them aware that our habitual train of thought is a cut above the pew level."

He goes on to say, "I could take a person with a high school education, give him or her a six-month trade school training, and provide a pastor who would be satisfactory to any discriminating American congregation."

Peterson believes that clergy have abandoned the three training practices basic to all pastoral work: the act of prayer, the reading of Scripture, and the practice of spiritual direction. He says, "Without these practices, there can be no developing substance — without these, the best of talents and best of intentions cannot prevent a thinning out into a life that becomes mostly impersonation."

He believes that the pastors of America have metamorphosed into a company of storekeepers preoccupied with keeping their customers happy while luring customers away from the competition down the street.[16]

What do you think about that? Is your refuge in God or in forms and images of religiosity?

DISAPPEARANCE

"The great use of life is
to spend it for something
that will outlast it."

Charles Mayes

*Listen to my cry for help, my King
and my God, for to you I pray.*

Psalm 5:2

An A-10 Thunderbolt II Air Force attack jet suddenly and mysteriously disappeared in the Colorado mountains in the spring of 1997. The pilot, Captain Craig Button, was also missing. With each passing day of thorough searching, the mystery surrounding the disappearance intensified. How could an $8.8 million Air Force attack jet just vanish?

As I kept up with the story, a parallel struck me. What about missing ministers? You may be one.

In our country today, there are scores of full-time and volunteer ministers who have just dropped off the radar screen. It may have been because they failed and were forced to go elsewhere. It might have been that life turned so sour, they just decided to become reclusive.

Maybe you have chosen to withdraw from those who care for you because it's just too difficult to be confronted with your calling and purpose.

We can't afford to lose another brother or sister! We must do all we can to locate those who have chosen to "get lost."

Unlimited resources were used to find the lost plane, and to date neither it nor the pilot have been located. Why is it that we do so little to locate and love back into the fold our colleagues? Is there someone you could reach out to today?

SIGNIFICANCE

"You matter to God!"

Then he looked at those seated in a circle around him and said, "Here are my mother and my brothers!"

Mark 3:34

In 1997 we observed both the 50th anniversary of Jackie Robinson crossing the color barrier into major league baseball (with the perpetual retirement of his number 42 throughout the league) and Tiger Woods' victory at one of golf's most historic arenas, the Masters at Augusta National Golf Club.

In doing so, Woods set a Masters' record of 18 under par. He also won $486,000 and, at 21, became the youngest champion in Masters' history. How did Tiger respond to this historic accomplishment? He said, "More than anything, I was relieved it was over. Every time I hug my mom and pop, I know [a tournament] is over and I've accomplished my goal. To share this with them is something special."

Notice he didn't say everytime he *wins,* he gets a hug. He said everytime he *completes a tournament,* he gets a hug.

Where do your hugs come from? A hug is symbolic of affection and gratitude. It's not about winning. It's all about trying and finishing.

I'm sure you may think at times that no one really cares, but I want you to know that WE CARE, and you are very important to us. In fact, if you were here right now, we would give you a great big hug!

It's just our way of saying thanks for all you do. You are a winner!

COMMUNICATION

"Communication is the
key to a great marriage!"

H. Norman Wright

Be completely humble and gentle;
be patient, bearing with
one another in love.

Ephesians 4:2

This might not apply to all of you, because it's about our kids. Neil Wiseman and I wrote in the book, *Pastors at Risk,* "Allow your children to see you as a human being who is hungry for God — something significantly different from being a religious professional."[17]

In one survey of ministers representing 32 denominations, 70 percent reported they work more than 60 hours per week, and 85 percent spend two or less evenings per week at home. That's a lot of time away from the family. And when they do get home, what do they have left to offer their loved ones?

We've found that the primary impediments to a healthy ministerial family are not church politics or environmental disadvantages. Rather, they stem from a lack of lived-out love and communication between the pastoral couple and their children.

Why not ask your wife and children how they feel about your schedule, and if they ever feel they take second place to the demands of the ministry? Find out if they think being a minister's family is a positive or negative experience.

If negative, help them work through their issues by listening, rather than preaching. When they are finished "letting it all out," instead of being defensive, ask them what they would like to see you do to remedy the situation. This may be your most informative and life-changing counseling session ever!

CALMNESS

"All is calm, all is bright."

"Silent Night"

*Let us fix our eyes on Jesus, the author
and perfecter of our faith, who for the
joy set before him endured the cross,
scorning its shame, and sat down at
the right hand of the throne of God.*

Hebrews 12:2

A good read for many of you is former president Jimmy Carter's book, *Living Faith*. It speaks candidly of the transformation of his religious beliefs into a living faith.

One particular statement in the book has stayed with me: "I see a number of times when what I believed I wanted most was challenged by a more difficult path. Whenever I had the courage to choose that path, even in the midst of despair and uncertainty, I was given a glimpse of deeper truths that continue to sustain me."[18]

What does that mean to you?

Let me share how it touches me — especially as a clergy colleague. There will be times when what we want, and even feel we deserve, is stalemated by the realities of life. However, that does not mean we should turn back or abandon our dreams, even for a moment.

Nothing can separate us from God's love or put us into a situation where He is helpless to hold us steady. In other words, God says, "Trust Me! Love Me! Believe in Me! I have you in the palm of My hand." *There I find calmness.*

The path you have chosen is not an easy one, but neither need it be a lonely one. For me, the joy we find is in the company we share, divine and human, and nothing can change that.

Jesus is faithful.

PASSION

"I once was lost,
but now I'm found!"

"Amazing Grace"

*How, then, can they call on the one
they have not believed in? And how can
they believe in the one of whom they
have not heard? And how can they hear
without someone preaching to them?
And how can they preach unless they are
sent? As it is written, "How beautiful
are the feet of those who bring good news!"*

Romans 10:14,15

When I spoke once at Southern Wesleyan University, the preliminaries were long and the room was warm. As the proceedings continued, I was led to change my message to a more passionate appeal for the lost to come to the saving grace of Jesus Christ.

While waiting, my thoughts had turned to a "drive thru" tour of another university. There, I had seen hundreds of students on that campus and was prompted by the Holy Spirit to wonder, "How many of these students know Jesus Christ as Savior?"

I was very emotional as I addressed the group at Southern Weslayan, because it dawned on me that in this world of "the church" we have a tendency to look more *at what we have, rather than what we don't have.* In the world that's okay, but in the kingdom of God I don't think it is.

There was a day in the church when the salvation message was the number one priority. I wonder if it still is. Is it with you?

The passion to lead the lost into a "found" condition must become paramount in all of our ministries if the nation and the world are to experience a genuine revival.

Endnotes

1   *Carpe Diem,* Tony Campolo (New York: HarperCollins/Zondervan, 1991) p. 100.

2   *My Utmost for His Highest,* Oswald Chambers (Westwood, NJ: Barbour Books, 1963) p. 170.

3   Adapted from *Who Switched the Price Tags?* Tony Campolo (Waco, TX: Word Books, 1986) pp. 109, 110.

4   *You Might Be a Preacher If...,* Stan Toler and Mark Toler Hollingsworth (Tulsa, OK: Albury Publishing, 1995) pp. 9-11, 21-23, 65, 71, 73, 90, 106, 138.

5   *On Being a Servant of God,* Warren Wiersbe (Nashville: Oliver-Nelson Books, a division of Thomas Nelson, Inc., 1993) p. 41.

6   *Experiencing God,* Henry T. Blackaby & Claude V. King (Nashville: Broadman and Holman, 1994).

7   *The Power of the Call,* Henry T. Blackaby, Henry Brandt & Kerry Skinner (Nashville: Broadman and Holman, 1997) p. 22 of unprinted manuscript.

8   *The Heart of a Great Pastor,* H. B. London Jr. & Neil B. Wiseman (Ventura, CA: Regal Books, 1994) p. 250.

9   *Your Pastor Is an Endangered Species — A Wake-Up Call to the Local Church,* H. B. London, Jr. & Neil B. Wiseman (Wheaton, IL: Victor Books, 1996) p. 42.

10 *God's Never Failed Me, But He's Sure Scared Me to Death a Few Times,* Stan Toler (Tulsa, OK: Honor Books, 1995) p. 141.

11 "Wonderful Peace," W. D. Cornell from *Praise & Worship* (Kansas City, MO: Lillenas Publishing Company, 1923) p. 334.

12 *Exhaustive Concordance of the Bible,* James Strong (Nashville: Abingdon, 1890) #3327, Hebrew and Chaldee Dictionary.

13 *More Than Conquerors — Portraits of Believers from All Walks of Life,* John Woodbridge, ed. (Chicago: The Moody Bible Institute of Chicago, 1992) p. 201.

14 *Prayer Shield,* Peter Wagner (Ventura, CA: Regal Books, a division of Gospel Light, 1992) p. 194.

[15] "Looking for Love," sung by Tommy Lee in the 1980 film, *Urban Cowboy.*

[16] *Working the Angles,* Eugene H. Peterson (Grand Rapids: Wm. B. Eerdmans Publishing Co., 1987) p. 4.

[17] *Pastors at Risk,* H. B. London, Jr. & Neil B. Wiseman (Wheaton, IL: Victor Books, 1993) p. 108.

[18] *Living Faith,* Jimmy Carter (New York: Times Books, a Division of Random House, 1996) back cover.

About The Author — H. B. London Jr.

H. B. London Jr., has pastored all of his adult life. Known as a gifted leader, pastor, and preacher, his ministry continues to be people-centered.

A fourth-generation minister, Rev. London was born in Little Rock, Arkansas, and is a graduate of Pasadena College (Point Loma College) and Nazarene Theological Seminary.

Dr. London is Vice-President of Ministry Outreach/Pastoral Ministries for Focus on the Family. He has directed the development of ministries to pastors and their spouses, and given oversight to ministries affecting physicians, crisis pregnancy centers, youth culture, the inner city, missionaries, chaplains, and basketball camps for children of single parents in cities throughout the United States and Canada. He communicates weekly with pastors and church leaders through "The Pastor's Weekly Briefing" (a fax network) and produces a bi-monthly "Pastor to Pastor" cassette and newsletter.

H. B. and his wife, Beverley, have two married sons and four grandchildren.

To write the author, address your correspondence to:

Dr. H. B. London Jr.
8605 Explorer Drive
Colorado Springs, Colorado 80920

About The Author — Stan Toler

Stan Toler has been encouraging people all his life. Known as a "pastor to pastors," a gifted leader, administrator, and inspirational speaker, Stan has given his life to seeing the kingdom of God grow with power and grace.

Stan was born in Welch, West Virginia, a small rural mountain community. By the time he was 15, he knew God wanted him to be a full-time minister. This was a role he adopted with youthful enthusiasm by becoming the pastor of Westside Church in Newark, Ohio, at age 17.

Stan has pastored some of the fastest-growing churches in the country, including Heritage Memorial Church (Ohio), Oklahoma City First Church of the Nazarene, and Nashville First Church of the Nazarene. He is currently the senior pastor of Trinity Nazarene Church in Oklahoma City and instructor for the INJOY Model Church Seminar.

Stan's wife, Linda (Carter), is an elementary school teacher. They have two sons, Seth Aaron and Adam James.

To write the author, address your correspondence to:

Dr. Stan Toler
P. O. Box 950
Bethany, Oklahoma 73008

Other published works and manuals by
H. B. London Jr. include:

Pastors at Risk

The Heart of a Great Pastor

Married to a Pastor's Wife

Your Pastor is an Endangered Species

It Takes a Church Within a Village

Refresh, Renew, Revive

Other published works and manuals by
Stan Toler include:

*God's Never Failed Me — But He's Sure
Scared Me To Death A Few Times*

Church Operations Manual

Minister's Little Instruction Book

ABC's of Evangelism

101 Ways to Grow A Healthy Sunday School

You Might Be A Preacher If...

Stewardship Starters

Minute Motivators

The People Principle

Additional copies of this book are available
from your local bookstore.

Honor Books
Tulsa, Oklahoma